Hieronymus Bosch:
110 Masterpieces

By Maria Tsaneva

First Edition

*****

I0477289

<u>**Hieronymus Bosch: 110 Masterpieces**</u>
*****

Foreword

Hieronymus Bosch's name derives from his birthplace, Hertogenbosch, which is usually pronounced "Den Bosch".

Bosch's left behind himself no correspondence or diaries, and what has been recognized has been in use from concise references to him in the community archives of Hertogenbosch. Not anything is identified of his character or his feelings on the significance of his painting. His birthday has not been determined with confidence. It is probable at c. 1450 on the starting point of his drawn portrait (may be a self-portrait?) made soon prior to his death in 1516. The depiction shows the man at an old age, most likely in his late sixties.

Bosch spent all his life in and close to Hertogenbosch, the principal of the Dutch county of Brabant. His grandfather Jan was also a painter and is mentioned in the city records in 1430. It is acknowledged that Jan had 5 sons, 4 of whom were as well painters. Bosch's father, Anthonius, served as art adviser to the Brotherhood of Our Lady, but however none of his works survive.

Bosch became a admired painter in his lifetime and frequently expected commissions. In 1488 Bosch joined the vastly valued Brotherhood of Our Lady, an super-conservative religious faction of a number of 40 powerful people of Hertogenbosch, and about 7 000 other members from Europe.

For a time stuck between 1479 and 1481, Bosch married Aleyt van den Meerveen, who was a few years older than him. The pair moved to the near Oirschot.

The archives of the Brotherhood of Our Lady report Bosch's death in 1516. A memorial service in his memory was held in the church of Saint John on 9-th August of the same year.

Bosch painted a number of triptychs. Amongst his mainly well-known is The Garden of Earthly Delights. This triptych depicts paradise with Adam and Eve and a lot of incredible animals on the left panel, the everyday delights with various naked figures and marvelous fruit and birds on the central panel, and hell with pictures of extraordinary tortures of the a range of types of sinners on the right side panel. When the external panels are closed the watcher can observe God creating the Earth. These triptychs have a rough surface, contrasts with the customary Flemish style, where the silky exterior attempts to hide from view the truth that the picture is made from man.

Hieronymus Bosch not at all dated his works and may have signed only few of them. Less than twenty five artworks stay today that can be recognized to him. Philip II of Spain acquired lot of Bosch's masterpieces after the Bosch's funeral; consequently, the Prado Museum now has several of his works, together with The Garden of Earthly Delights.

In the past it was habitually supposed that Bosch's paintings was inspired by medieval heresies and unclear enclosed practices. Some others consideration is that his art was formed just to shock and entertain much similar to the "grotteschi" of the Italian Renaissance. Despite the fact that the art of the older masters was founded in the material world of daily practice, Bosch attacks his watcher by way of "a world of dreams and nightmares in which forms seem to flash and transform ahead of our eyes." In the primary identified description of Bosch's artworks, in 1560 Felipe de Guevara wrote that Bosch was regarded simply as "the originator of monsters and chimeras". In the beginning 17-th century, the Dutch Karel van Mander explained Bosch's art as "marvelous and extraordinary fantasies"; nevertheless, he finished that the paintings are "frequently less enjoyable than frightening to look at."

In the 20-th century, researchers have come to sight Bosch's vision as fewer unbelievable, and acknowledged that his art reflects the conventional religious faith systems of his time. His images of sinning people, his view of Heaven and Hell are now perceived as consistent with those of late medieval didactic literature and habits. It is in the main acknowledged that Bosch's art was produced to educate exact moral and spiritual norms, and that his images provide precise worth.

Nerveless, some critics notice Bosch as example of medieval surrealist, and parallels are repeatedly made with the modern Spanish artist Salvador Dali. Other scholars try to interpret his images using the words of Freudian psychology.

The correct number of Bosch's existing artworks has been a topic of substantial dispute. He signed only 7 of his paintings, and there is doubt whether every one the paintings on one occasion ascribed to him were in fact from his hand. In adding up, his technique was very high-ranking, and was extensively imitated by his various followers. Nowadays no more than 25 masterpieces are definitively credited to him.

Paintings and Drawings

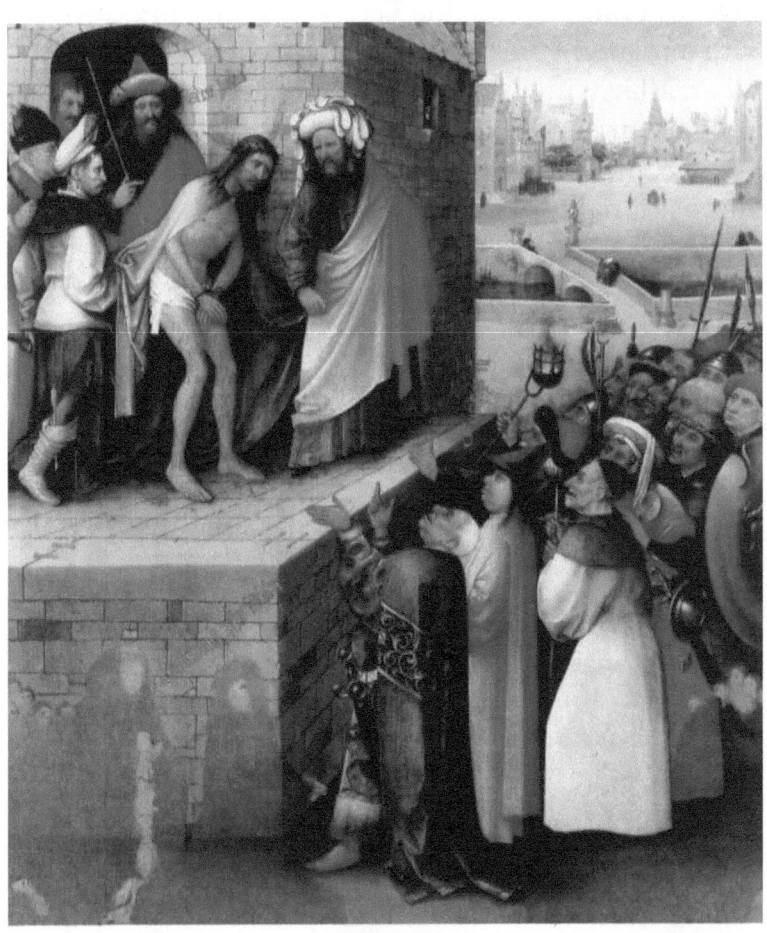

Ecce Homo
1475-80, Tempera and oil on oak panel, 71 x 61 cm

Among the works generally ascribed to Bosch's first period of activity (c. 1470-85) may be included several small biblical scenes: the Epiphany (Adoration of the Magi) in Philadelphia, the Ecce Homo in Frankfurt (with a related version in Boston, Museum of Fine Arts) and an altar wing in Vienna, the Christ Carrying the Cross. Their early date is suggested by their relatively simple compositions and their adherence to traditional compositional types.

In the Ecce Homo, crowned with thorns and his flesh beaten raw by the scourge, Christ stands with Pilate and his companions before the angry mob. The dialogue between Pilate and the crowd is indicated by the Gothic inscriptions. From the mouth of Pilate issue the words Ecce Homo (Behold the Man). There is no need to decipher the inscription Crufige Eum (Crucify Him), the cry which rises from the people below; their animosity is unmistakably conveyed by their facial expressions and threatening gestures. The third inscription Salve nos Christe redemptor (Save us, Christ Redeemer) once emerged from two donors at lower left, but their figures have been painted over. The heathen character of the men surrounding Christ is suggested by their strange dress and headgear, including pseudo-oriental turbans. The scene's essential wickedness is further indicated by such traditional emblems of evil as the owl in the niche above Pilate and the giant toad sprawled on the back of a shield carried by one of the soldiers. In the background appears a city square, the Turkish crescent fluttering from one of its towers. The enemies of Christ have been identified with the power of Islam which in Bosch's day, and long afterwards, controlled the most holy places of Christendom. The buildings, however, are late Gothic; only the oddly bulging tower in the distance evokes a feeling of far-off places.

The Dutch character of this early work is unmistakable. The homely faces and animated gestures of Christ's tormentors recall Passion scenes in Dutch manuscripts of the second and third quarters of the fifteenth century, where we encounter similar physical types, slight in proportion, flatly modelled and often unsubstantial beneath their heavy robes.

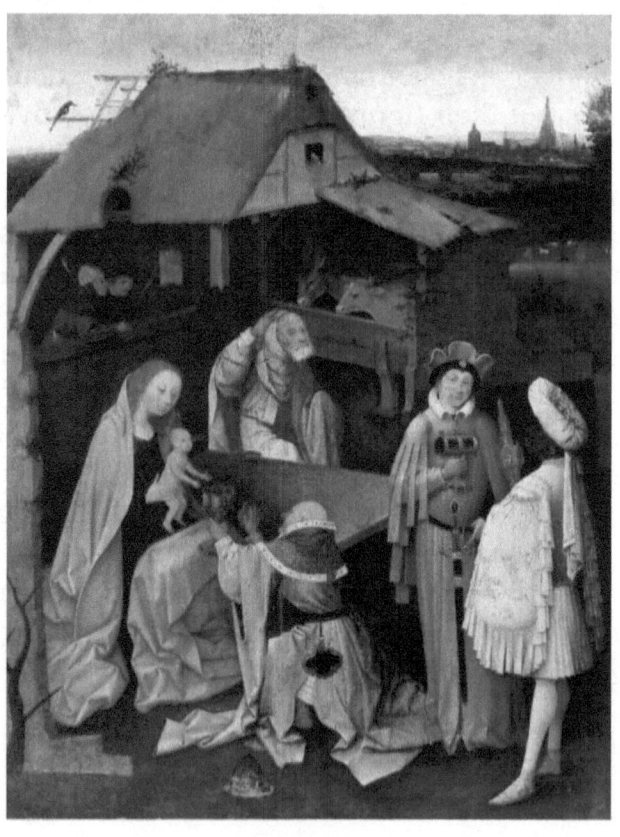

Epiphany
1475-80, Oil on panel, 74 x 54 cm

The early style is especially well exemplified in the charming Epiphany« in Philadelphia. The dignified comportment of the Kings is set off by the impulsive gesture of the Christ Child, while the aged Joseph stands discreetly to one side, removing his hood as if abashed by the presence of the splendidly dressed strangers. From behind the shed two shepherds look on with shy curiosity. At this early date, Bosch's grasp of perspective was apparently none too firm; particularly ambiguous is the spatial relationship of the stable to the figures in the foreground, although the crumbling walls and thatched roof have been painted with a loving attention to detail. In the distance at the upper right can be seen a pasture filled with grazing cattle and the shimmering towers of a city.

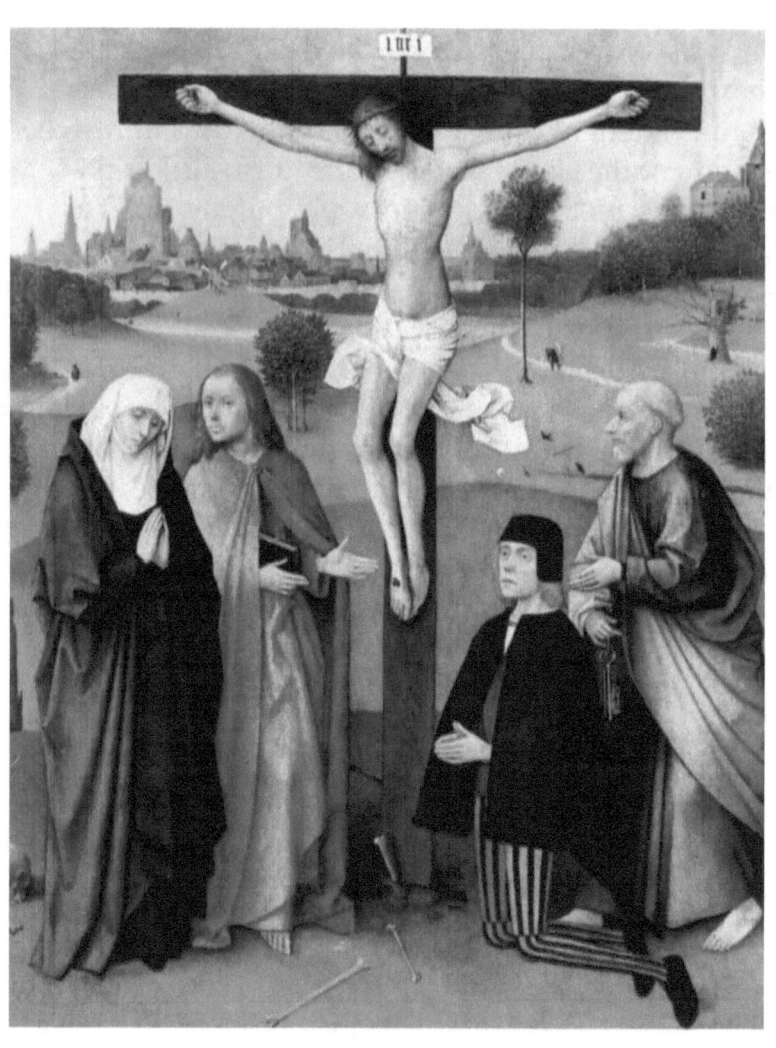

Crucifixion with a Donor
1480-85, Oil on oak, 74, 7 x 61 cm

Hieronymus Bosch lived and worked at 'Hertogenbosch where he was born into a family of artists coming originally from Aachen. He was introduced into high society, where he received commissions from prestigious persons. He is known for his works peopled with demonic beings, revealing an exceptional independence from the pictorial tradition of his time. However, the Crucifixion with a Donor, which is attributed to him, is perfectly in line with the iconographic tradition of the 15th century.

The composition shows a sort of hierarchical intercession procedure. The kneeling donor is praying for his salvation. He is accompanied by his patron, St Peter, identified by the key in his hand. Turning towards St John the Evangelist, St Peter presents his protйgй. St John then looks towards the Virgin, asking her to intercede with her Son, which she does by praying. Christ figures on the cross as a sign of redemption, his sacrifice having made possible the salvation of the human race. The scene is portrayed in the place reserved for the torture of condemned criminals, on the edge of a Brabant city which is visible in the distance. Midway, a broken gibbet lies on the ground, surrounded by scattered bones and crows. Some figures are walking along the paths leading towards a mill to the left and a castle to the right.

The donor's identity is not known. Only his first name, Peter, is indicated by the presence of his patron saint. He is dressed in a white shirt and a brown pourpoint. Over this he wears a black cape and a hat on his head. His legs are dressed in striped black and red breeches and stockings decorated with the same motif. A sword shows out from under the cape. This costume, which was worn in the Low Countries during the last 20 years of the 15th century, could indicate that the donor was in a lord's service.

We do not know whether this panel originally had wings. No other crucifixion by Hieronymus Bosch is known, although the theme returns as a secondary motif in others of his paintings. It is also one of the master's few works containing a donor portrait. The style displays a striking balance and serenity. The flesh colours of Christ's body are softened and the draperies sober. The countryside shows a very gentle gradation of greens, producing a successful effect of depth.

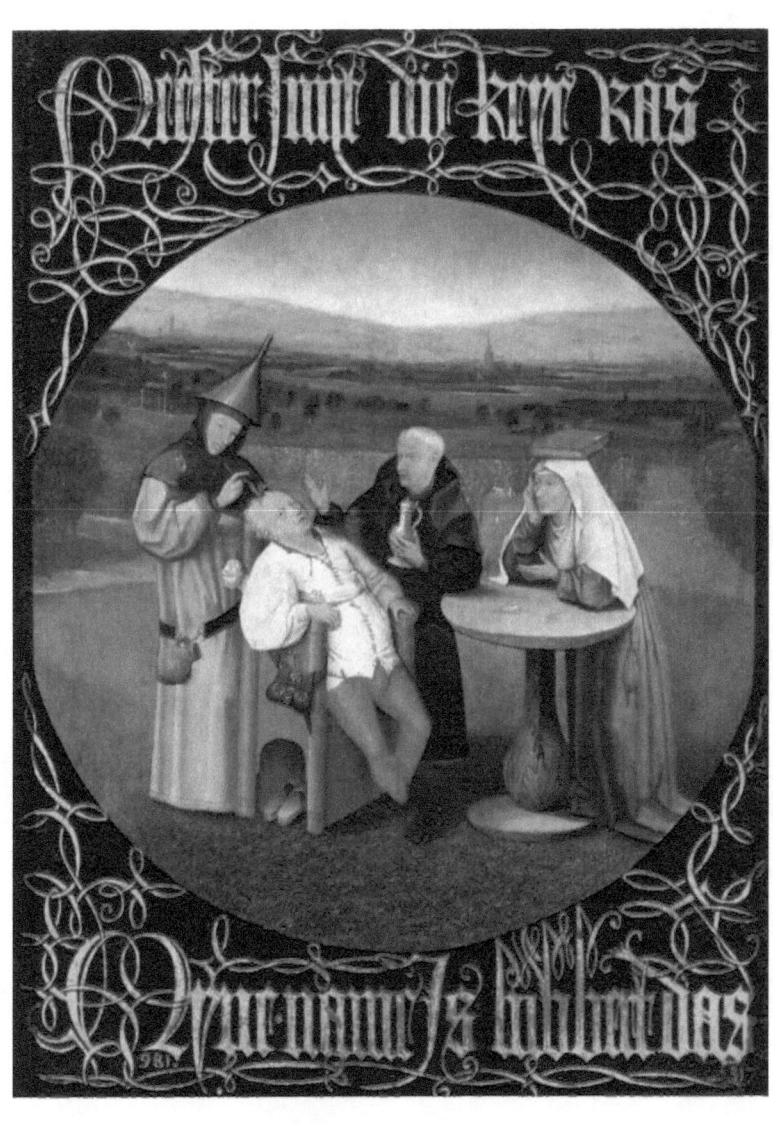

The Cure of Folly (Extraction of the Stone of Madness)
1475-80, Oil on panel, 48 x 35 cm

In the midst of a luxuriant summer landscape, a surgeon removes an object from the head of a man tied to a chair; a monk and a nun look on. This little picture may not be entirely by Bosch; the awkward and inexpressive figures are perhaps by an inferior hand, but only Bosch could have been responsible for the landscape background whose delicately painted forms recall the vista in his early Epiphany. The open-air operation, its circular shape suggesting a mirror, is set within a framework of elaborate calligraphical decoration containing the inscription: "Master, cut the stone out, my name is Lubbert Das."

In Bosch's day, the stone operation was a piece of quackery in which the patient was supposedly cured of his stupidity through the removal of the stone of folly from his forehead. Fortunately, it was performed only in fiction, not in fact, for in literary examples of this theme it generally left the patient worse off than before. The name "Lubbert", on the other hand, frequently appears in Dutch literature to designate persons exhibiting an unusually high degree of human stupidity. The stone operation was occasionally represented by later Netherlandish artists, including Pieter Bruegel the Elder. This subject undoubtedly inspired Bosch's picture, but no extant version of it accounts for the funnel and the book perched on the heads of two of the characters, nor does it explain the presence of the monk and the nun, although their apparent acquiescence in the quackery certainly places them in an unfavourable light. It will be noted, too, that what the surgeon extracts from Lubbert's head is not a stone, but a flower; another flower of the same species lies on the table at the right. The flowers have identified as tulips and their presence is explained as a play on the Dutch word for tulip which in the sixteenth century also carried the connotation of stupidity and folly.

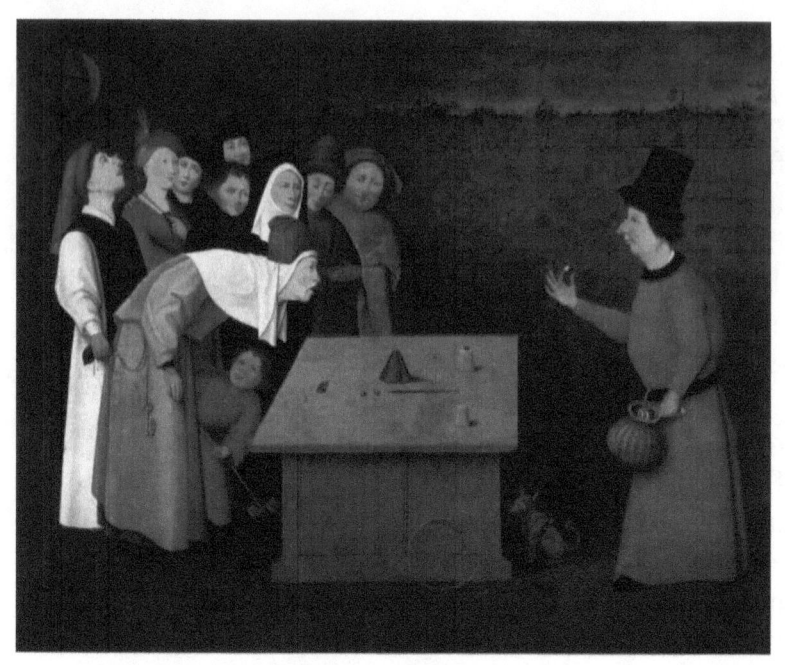

The Magician
1475-80, Oil on panel, 53 x 75 cm

The Magician belonging to Bosch's early paintings is now lost but it is known through a faithful copy at Saint-Germain-en-Laye. A mountebank has set up his table before a crumbling stone wall. His audience watches spellbound as he seems to bring forth a frog from the mouth of an old man in their midst; only one of the crowd, the young man with his hand on the shoulder of his female companion, appears to notice that the old man's purse is being stolen by the conjuror's confederate. The myopic gaze of the thief and the stupid amazement of the frog-spitting victim are superbly played off against the amused reactions of the bystanders, while the slyness of the mountebank is well conveyed in his sharp-nosed physiognomy. Bosch exploits the human face in profile for expressive purposes. Although the painting may possess a moralizing significance, it must have been inspired by a real-life situation closely observed. The perceptive, spontaneous humour of this little picture would be difficult to match in contemporary Flemish painting, but parallels can be found among Dutch manuscript illuminators.

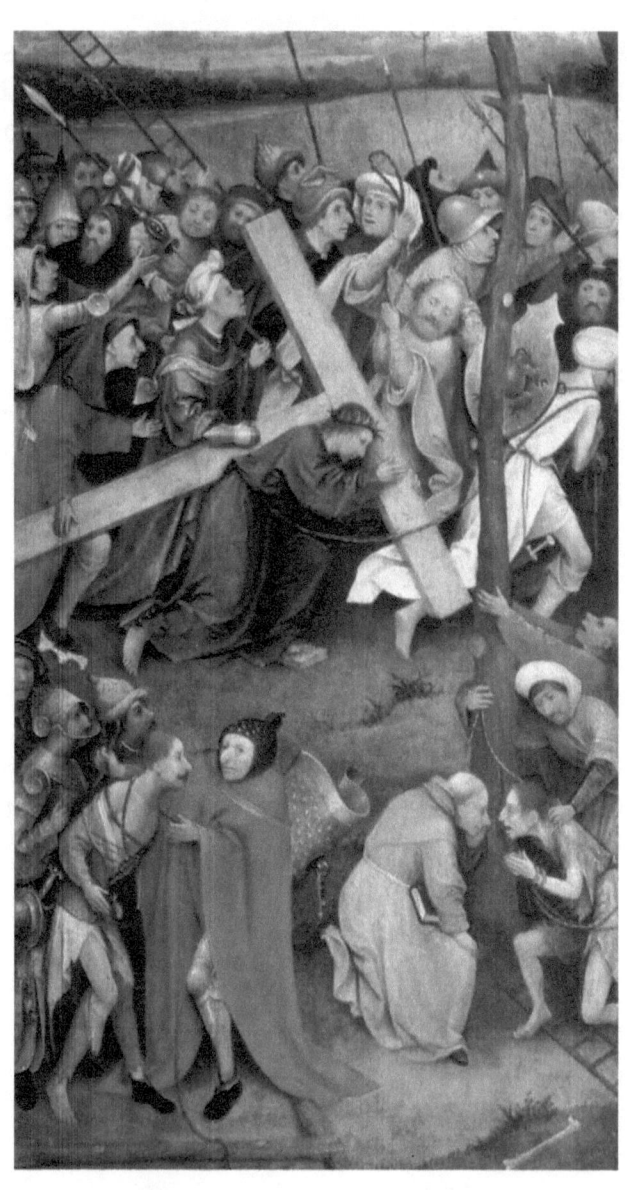

Christ Carrying the Cross
1480s, Oil on panel, 57 c 32 cm

In the Christ Carrying the Cross, the head of Christ is silhouetted against a dense mass of grimacing soldiers and ill-wishers, one of them bearing the familiar toad on his shield. Christ's physical agony is heightened by the spike-studded wooden blocks which dangle fore and aft from his waist, lacerating his feet and ankles with every step. This cruel device was frequently represented by Dutch artists well into the sixteenth century. The high horizon is old-fashioned, as is the lack of spatial recession in the middle distance. In the foreground, soldiers torment the bad thief while the good thief kneels before a priest. The almost frantic intensity of his confession, well-expressed by the open-mouthed profile, contrasts vividly with the passive response of the priest who seems to suppress a yawn. The very presence of the priest is, of course, an anachronism, probably inspired by what Bosch had witnessed at contemporary executions; the same motif appears in the great multi-figure Christ Carrying the Cross which Pieter Bruegel the Elder was to paint almost a century later.

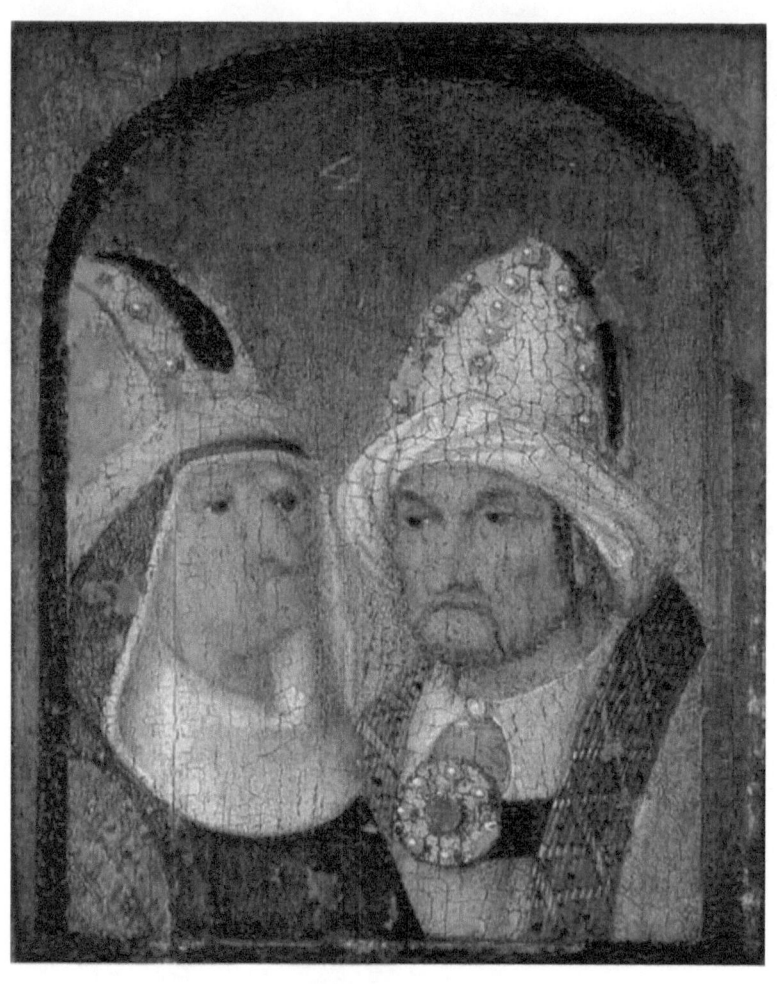

Two Male Heads
1480s, Oil on panel, 14, 5 x 12 cm

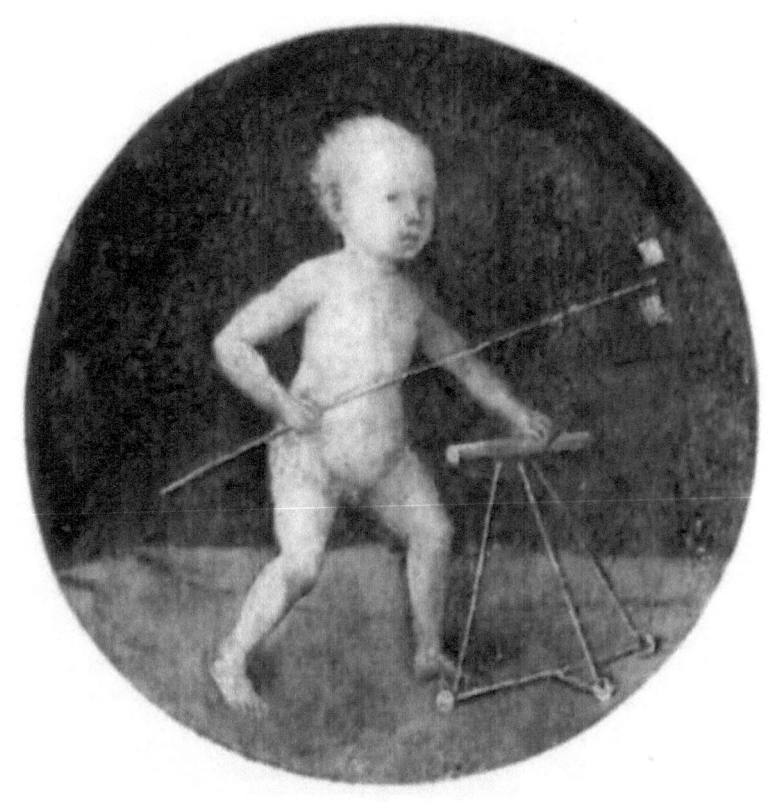

Christ Child with a Walking Frame
1480s, Oil on panel, diameter 28 cm

This rather unusual painting on the reverse of the Christ Carrying the Cross depicts a naked child pushing a walking-frame. This is the Christ Child, whose first halting steps clearly parallel Christ struggling with his Cross on the obverse, while the toy windmill or whirligig clutched in his hand probably alludes to the Cross itself. Thus Bosch gives us a touching picture of Christ in all his human frailty as he begins the road to his Passion.

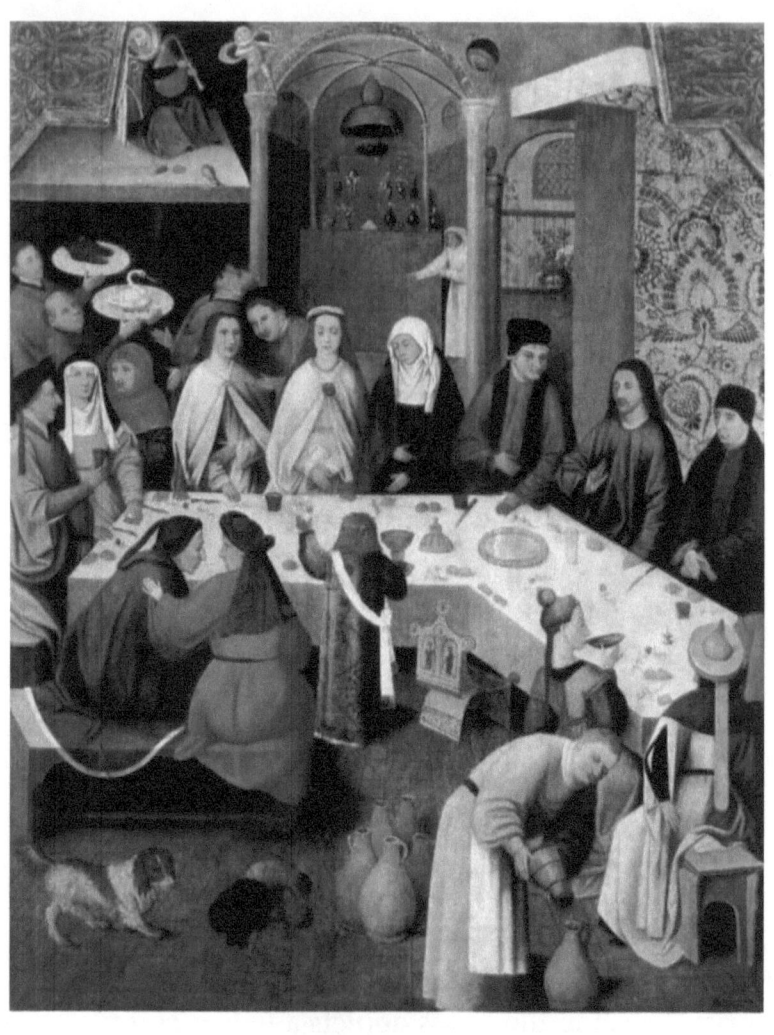

Marriage Feast at Cana
1480s, Oil on panel, 93 x 72 cm

The Marriage Feast at Cana was painted towards the end of Bosch's early period. The picture is not in good condition; the upper corners have been cut off, many heads have been repainted, and a pair of dogs at the lower left may have been added as late as the eighteenth century.

The marriage banquet has been placed in a richly furnished interior, most probably a tavern. The miracle of the wine jars takes place at lower right; the guests are seated around an L-shaped table dominated at one end by the figure of Christ, behind who hangs the brocaded cloth of honour usually reserved for the bride; he is flanked by two male donors in contemporary dress. Next to the Virgin at the centre of the table appear the solemn, austerely clad bridal couple; the bridegroom must be John the Evangelist, for his face closely resembles the type which Bosch employed elsewhere for this saint. Although the bridegroom remains nameless in the New Testament account, he was frequently identified as Christ's most beloved disciple.

Christ and his friends are pensively absorbed in some inner vision, unaware of the evil enchantment which seems to have fallen upon the banquet hall. The other wedding guests drink or gossip, watched by the bagpiper who leers drunkenly from a platform at the upper left. On the columns flanking the rear portal, two sculptured demons have mysteriously come to life; one aims an arrow at the other who escapes by disappearing through a hole in the wall. From the left, two servants carry in a boar's head and a swan spitting fire from their mouths; an ancient emblem of Venus, the swan symbolized unchastity. This unholy revelry seems to be directed by the innkeeper or steward who stands with his baton in the rear chamber. On the sideboard next to him are displayed curiously formed vessels, some of which, like the pelican, are symbolic of Christ, while others possess less respectable connotations, such as the three naked dancers on the second shelf.

The precise meaning of all these details remains unclear, as does that of the richly gowned child, his back turned to the viewer, who seems to toast the bridal couple with a chalice. However this may be, Bosch has undoubtedly employed the tavern setting as an image of evil, a comparison popular in medieval sermons, thereby contrasting the chaste marriage feast at Cana with the debauchery of the world.

In its transformation of a biblical story, the Marriage Feast of Cana introduces us for the first time to the complexity of Bosch's thought. It presents, on the one hand, a moral allegory of man's pursuit of the flesh at the expense of his spiritual welfare, and on the other, the monastic ideal of a life secure from the world in contemplation of God. These two themes were to dominate almost all Bosch's later art.

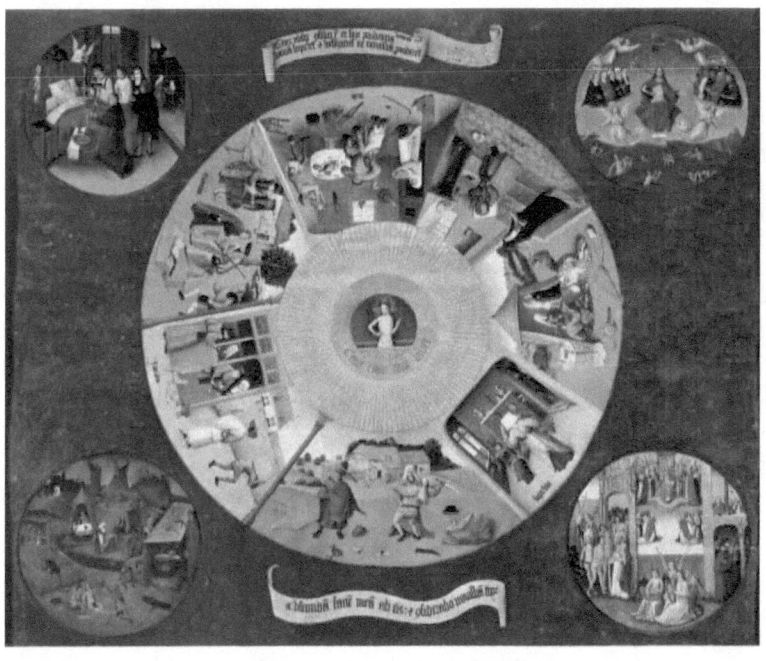

The Seven Deadly Sins
c. 1480, Oil on panel, 120 x 150 cm

This is one of Bosch's earliest known works and reflects the style and preoccupation which would later come to be considered characteristic of him. It belonged to Philip II King of Spain, who kept it in his apartments at the monastery of the Escorial.

The Seven Deadly Sins is a painted rectangle with a central image of the eye of God with Christ watching the world. The Seven Deadly Sins, depicted through scenes of worldly transgression, are arranged around the circular shape. The circular layout with God in the centre represents God's all Seeing Eye: No sin goes unnoticed. In the corners of the image appear the "Four Last Things" (the last four stages of life) mentioned in late medieval spiritual handbooks: Deathbed, Last Judgment, Heaven, and Hell, all of which are favourite themes of separate Bosch panels.

In the centre, fanned out around the figure of Christ, appear seven scenes each illustrating one of the Seven Deadly Sins, bearing the appropriate inscription and composed with the painter's usual vivacity and sense of the fantastic. (1) Anger presents a scene of jealousy and conflict; (2) in Pride, a demon presents a woman with a mirror; (3) in Lust, two sets of lovers speak within the confines of an open tent, entertained by a buffoon, while on the ground outside lie various musical instruments, including a harp which will reappear in the 'Garden of Earthly Delights'; (4) Idleness is represented by a woman dressed up for church and trying to wake a man deep in slumber; (5) Gluttony shows a table spread with food and around it figures eating voraciously; (6) Avarice displays a judge allowing himself to be bribed; and (7) Envy depicts the Flemish proverb 'Two dogs with one bone seldom reach agreement'.

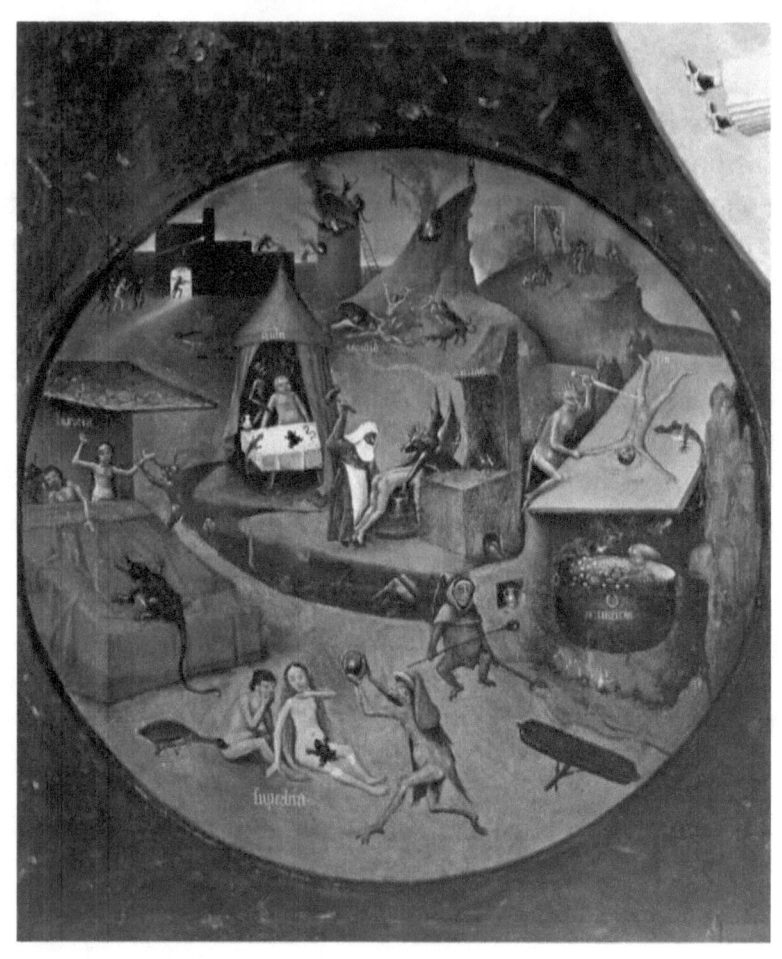

The Seven Deadly Sins (detail)
c. 1480, Oil on panel, diameter of detail: 36, 3 cm
The detail represents the Hell, one of the four tondos.

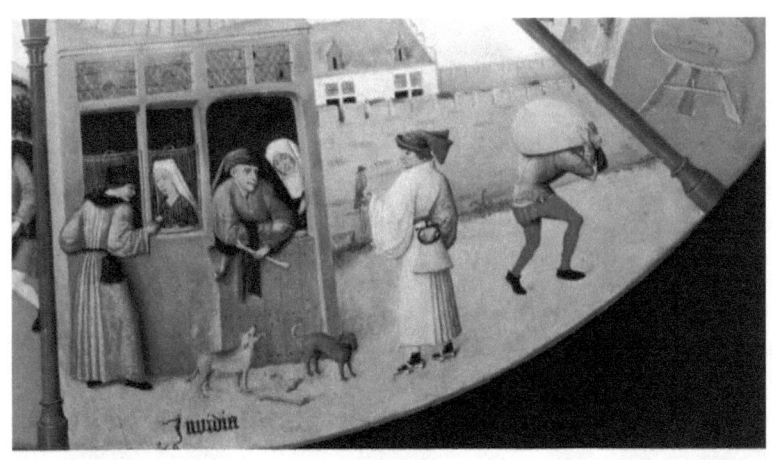

The Seven Deadly Sins (detail)
c. 1480, Oil on panel, width of detail 49 cm

The detail represents Envy, one of the seven deadly sins. In this scene the husband and wife are compared to the dogs below, who ignore the bones within their reach in favour of another held by the man. Their daughter has a perfectly adequate suitor, to judge by his ample purse; however, the parents look longingly at the stylish gentleman, who has others do his work.

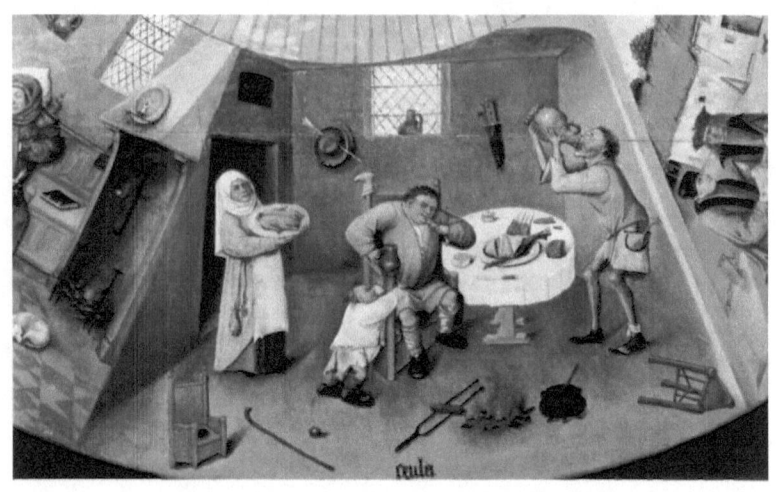

The Seven Deadly Sins (detail)
c. 1480, Oil on panel, width of detail 43, 5 cm

The detail represents Gluttony, one of the seven deadly sins. A father and son satisfy their gluttonous urgings. As they staff themselves, a child defecates in his clothes.

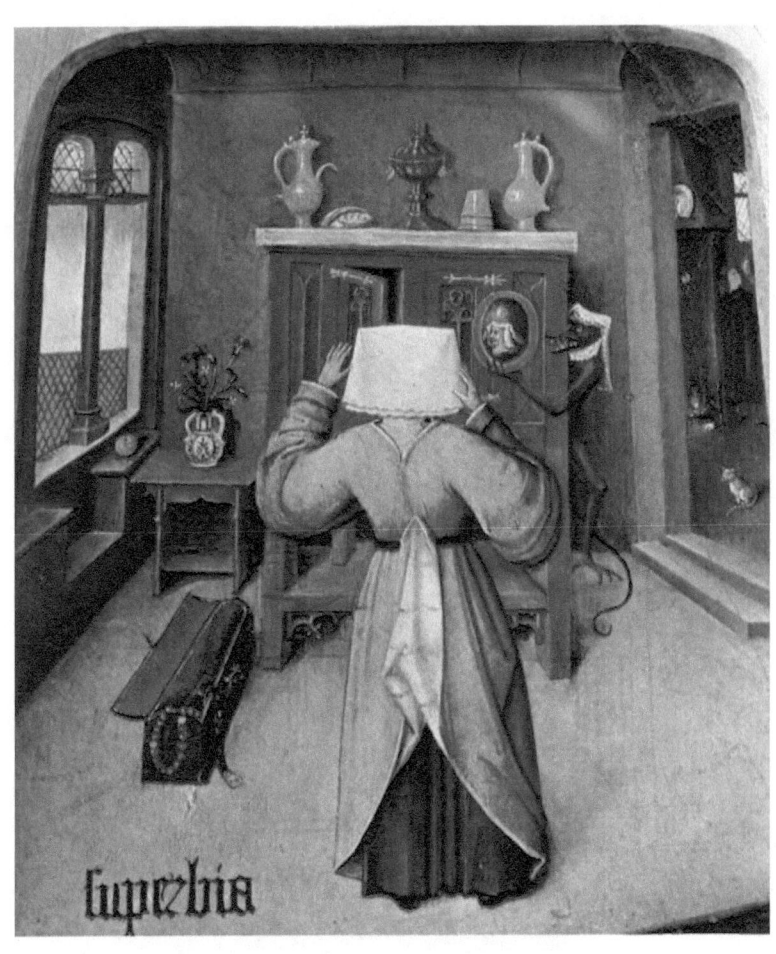

The Seven Deadly Sins (detail)
c. 1480, Oil on panel, width of detail 23 cm

The detail represents Vanity, one of the seven deadly sins. A wealthy woman, surrounded by her abundant material possessions, stares into a mirror as she adjusts her headdress. She fails to recognize that a devil, sporting a similar cloth headpiece, holds her mirror.

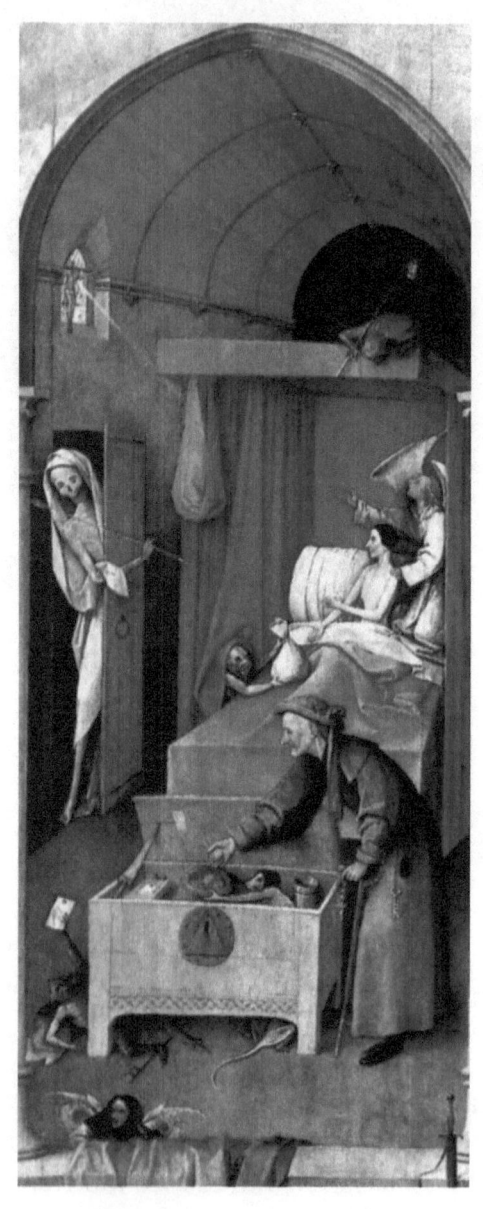

Death and the Miser
c. 1490, Oil on wood, 93 x 31 cm

That man persists in his folly even at the moment of death, when the eternities of Heaven and Hell hang in the balance, is the subject of the Death and the Miser. The dying man lies in a high, narrow bedchamber, into which Death has already entered at the left. His guardian angel supports him and attempts to draw his attention to the crucifix in the window above, but he is still distracted by the earthly possessions he must leave behind; one hand reaches out almost automatically to clutch the bag of gold offered by a demon through the curtain. Another demon, delicately winged, leans on the ledge in the foreground, where the rich robes and knightly equipment probably allude to the worldly rank and power which the miser must also abandon.

The battle of angels and devils for the soul of the dying man occurs also in the Prado "Tabletop" (where the traditional figure of Death armed with an arrow likewise appears), and both scenes reflect a popular fifteenth-century devotional work, the Ars Moriendi or Craft of Dying, which was printed many times in Germany and the Netherlands. This curious little handbook describes how the dying man is exposed to a series of temptations by the demons clustered around his bed and how, each time, an angel consoles him and strengthens him in his final agony. In this book, the angel is ultimately successful and the soul is carried victoriously to Heaven as the devils howl in despair below. In Bosch's painting, however, the issue of the struggle is far from certain. An opened money chest can be seen at the foot of the bed, where an elderly man, perhaps the miser shown a second time, places a gold piece into a bag held by a demon. He seems little concerned with the rosary hanging from his waist.

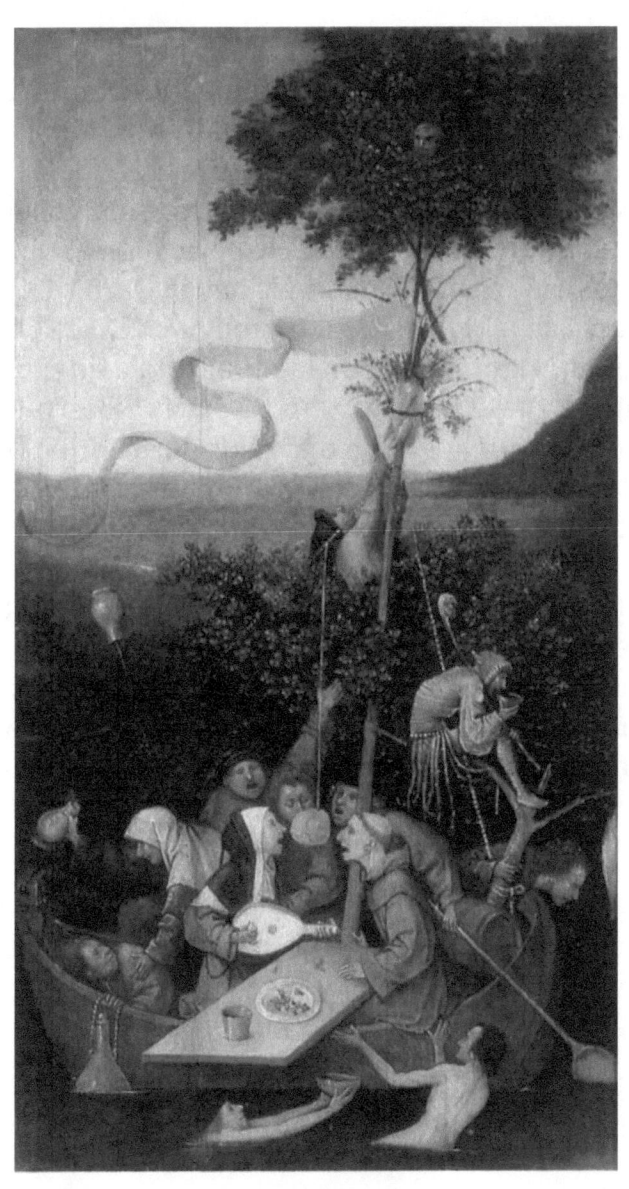

The Ship of Fools
1490-1500, Oil on wood, 58 x 33 cm

In The Ship of Fools " Bosch is imagining that the whole of mankind is voyaging through the seas of time on a ship, a small ship, that is representative of humanity. Sadly, every one of the representatives is a fool. This is how we live, says Bosch--we eat, dring, flirt, cheat, play silly games, pursue unattainable objectives. Meanwhile our ship drifts aimlessly and we never reach the harbour. The fools are not the irreligious, since promiment among them are a monk and a nun, but they are all those who live ``in stupidity". Bosch laughs, and it is sad laugh. Which one of us does not sail in the wretched discomfort of the ship of human folly? Eccentric and secret genius that he was, Bosch not only moved the heart but scandalized it into full awareness. The sinister and monstrous things that he brought forth are the hidden creatures of our inward self-love: he externalizes the ugliness within, and so his misshapen demons have an effect beyond curiosity. We feel a hateful kinship with them. "The Ship of Fools" is not about other people, it is about us.

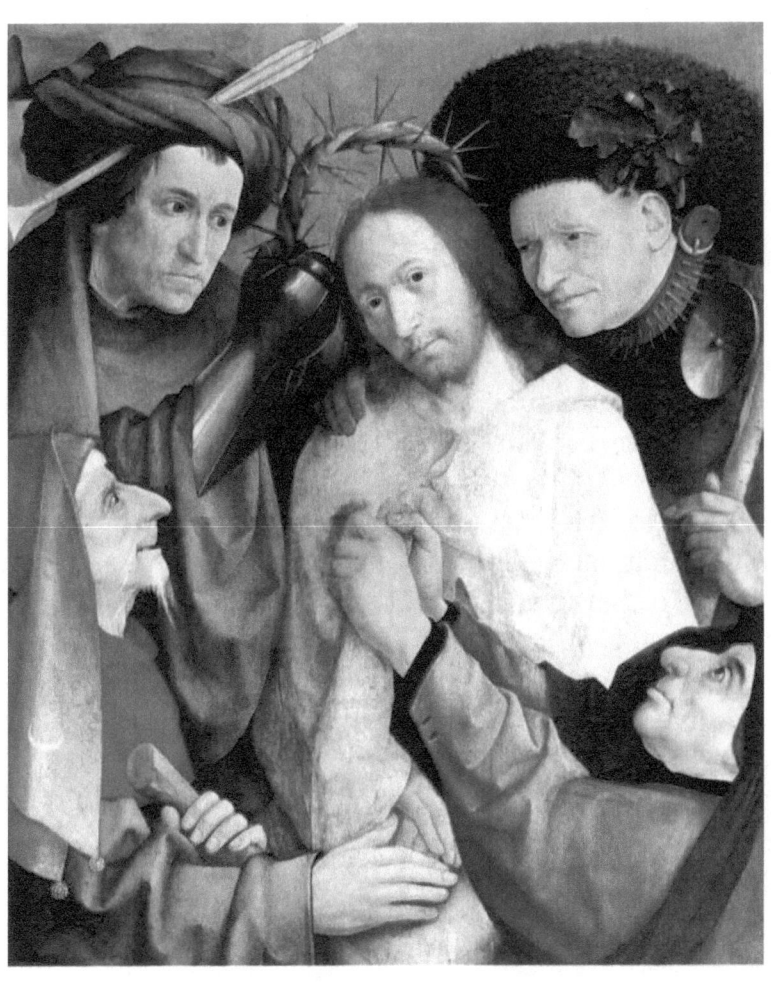

Christ Mocked (Crowning with Thorns)
1495-1500, Oil on wood, 73 x 59 cm

Bosch painted a group of half-length Passion scenes. The earliest example most probably is the Christ Crowned with Thorns in London. The large, firmly modelled figures are composed against the plain, grey-blue background with the utmost simplicity, the white-robed Christ surrounded by his four tormentors. One soldier holds a crown of thorns above his head, other tugs at his robe, and a third touches his hand with a mocking gesture. Their actions, however, seem curiously ineffectual and Christ ignores his persecutors to look calmly, even gently, at the spectator.

The half-length format and the tendency to crowd the figures against the picture plane with little indication of space are characteristics which reflect a Flemish devotional type popularized by Hugo van der Goes and Hans Memling. Like its Flemish models, the London Christ Crowned with Thorns presents the sacred scene not in its historical actuality but in its timeless aspect.

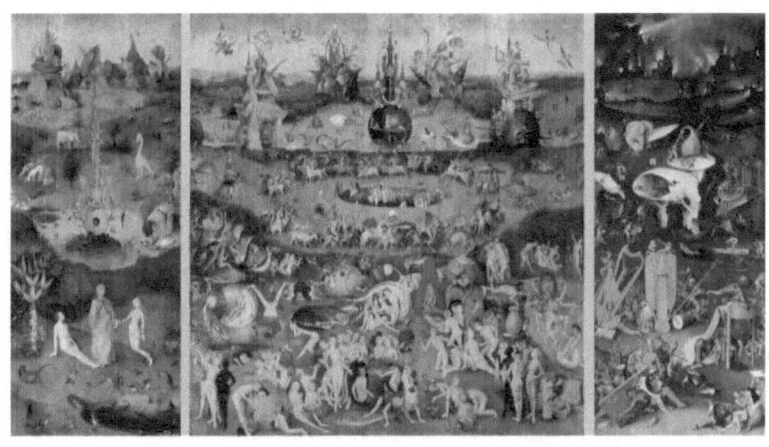

Triptych of Garden of Earthly Delights
c. 1500, Oil on panel, central panel: 220 x 195 cm,
wings: 220 x 97 cm

This painting is one of the most enigmatic pictures ever
made; it has captivated and puzzled audiences since its
inception. It is a large triptych, yet it was never
destined for a religious setting. It is a conversation
piece that is it is a picture intended to be closely viewed
and its meaning discussed among friends or visitors. It
can be read on many levels, from the literal to the
allegorical.

The closed position depicts the Earth on the third day of Creation; the muted grey-green of the exterior contrasts vividly with the vibrant colours of the three interior panels. Reading from left to right, the interior begins with paradise. As Christ prepares to wed Adam and Eve, he direct his glance and blessing to the viewer. Bosch's Garden of Eden is filled with real and fantastic creatures, verdant meadows, anthropomorphic rocks and bizarre hillocks, part pod and part crystal. Above Christ is a fountain of life.

The landscape and perspective schemes of the left and central scenes are identical. The garden is filled with young men and women of many races. There are no children and no older adults. Adam and Eve's progeny frolic unselfconsciously. Some kiss or engage in more amorous activities, others converse or eat strawberries and various fruits. A cavalcade of male riders encircles a group of bathing women in the middle third of the picture. The lack of a clear focal point or linear narrative makes the central panel the hardest to understand.

By contrast, the right wing is hell, and it finds its counterparts in other Bosch pictures. Divided into three tiers, hell includes a blasted landscape exploding in flames and smoke. A windmill is powered by sails of infernal light.. Great crowds march endlessly. In the middle, some figures skate on thin ice. A bizarre tree-man dominates. His shell-like torso forms a tavern, while couples, each comprised of one human and one demon, dance on his head to a bagpipe's melody. He looks furtively rather than directly at the viewer. The foreground is cluttered with punishments for the seven deadly sins. The prideful woman will spend eternity staring at her reflection mirrored in the backside of a devil, whose hand-like roots fondle her body. Gluttons are consumed, while a miser excretes gold coins into a cesspool. The hunters are now hunted, as indicated by the rabbit with his quarry, in this world upside down. An amorous sow, wearing the headdress of a Dominican nun, attempts to seduce the man at the lower right into signing the legal document.

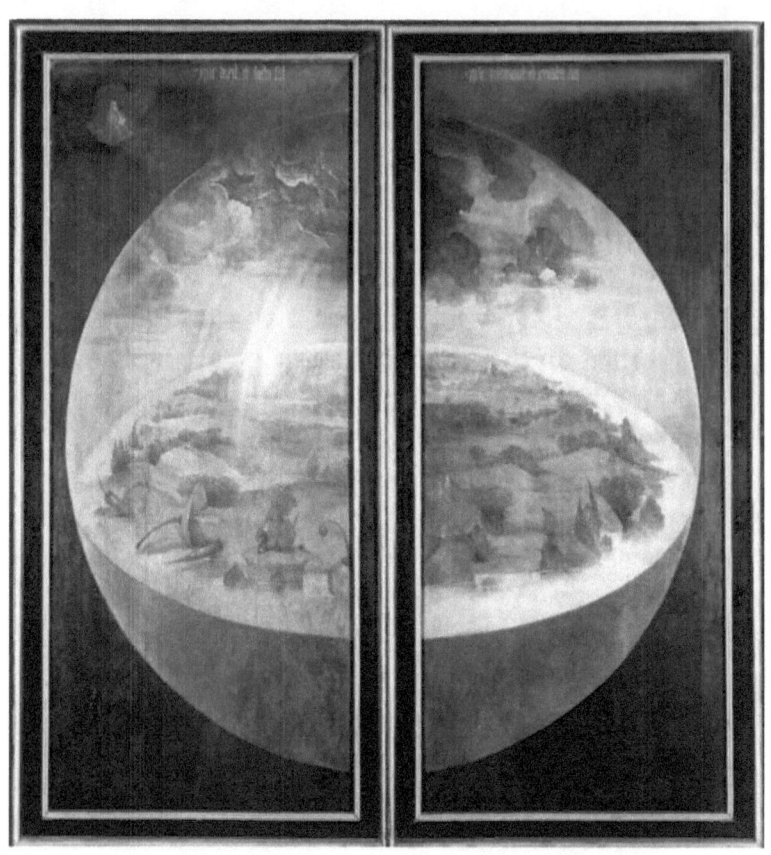

Triptych of Garden of Earthly Delights (outer wings)
c. 1500, Oil on panel, 220 x 97 cm (each wing)

The message of this panel can be understood from the moralizing content of the entire triptych. When the triptych is closed, it depicts the third day of Creation. The globe is contained in an opaque crystal sphere, symbolizing the fragility and transitoriness of the human world. When opened, the left side-panels reveal scenes from the Garden of Eden, the first human couple, the creation of Eve; in the centre is the fantastic vision of sensual pleasures, while the right panel shows the atonement of the damned in hell.

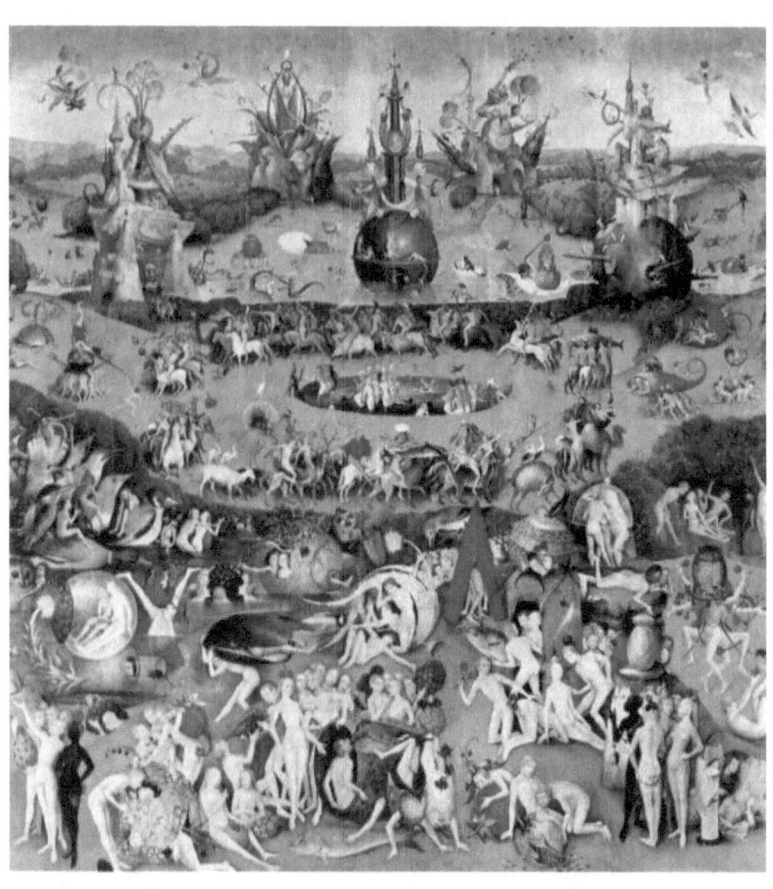

Triptych of Garden of Earthly Delights (central panel)
c. 1500, Oil on panel, 220 x 195 cm

At first sight, the central panel confronts us with an idyll unique in Bosch's work: an extensive park-like landscape teeming with nude men and women who nibble at giant fruits, consort with birds and animals, frolic in the water and, above all, indulge in a variety of amorous sports overtly and without shame. A circle of male riders revolves like a great carousel around a pool of maidens in the centre and several figures soar about in the sky on delicate wings. This triptych is better preserved than most of Bosch's large altarpieces, and the carefree mood of the central panel is heightened by the clear and even lighting, the absence of shadows, and the bright, high-keyed colours. The pale bodies of the inhabitants, accented by an occasional black-skinned figure, gleam like rare flowers against the grass and foliage. Behind the gaily coloured fountains and pavilions of the background lake, a soft line of hills melts into the distance. The diminutive figures and the large, fanciful vegetable forms seem as harmless as the medieval ornament which undoubtedly inspired them. We might be in the presence of the childhood of the world, when men and beasts dwelt in peace together and the earth yielded her fruit abundantly and without effort.

Nevertheless, this crowd of naked lovers was not intended as an apotheosis of innocent sexuality. The sexual act, which the twentieth century has learned to accept as a normal part of the human condition, was most often seen by the Middle Ages as proof of man's fall from the state of angels, at best a necessary evil, at worst a deadly sin. That Bosch shared fully in this view is confirmed by the fact that his garden, like the haywain in his other triptych, is situated between Eden and Hell, the origin of sin and its punishment. Hence, just as the Haywain depicts worldly gain or Avarice, so the Garden of Earthly Delights depicts the sensual life, more specifically the deadly sin of Lust.

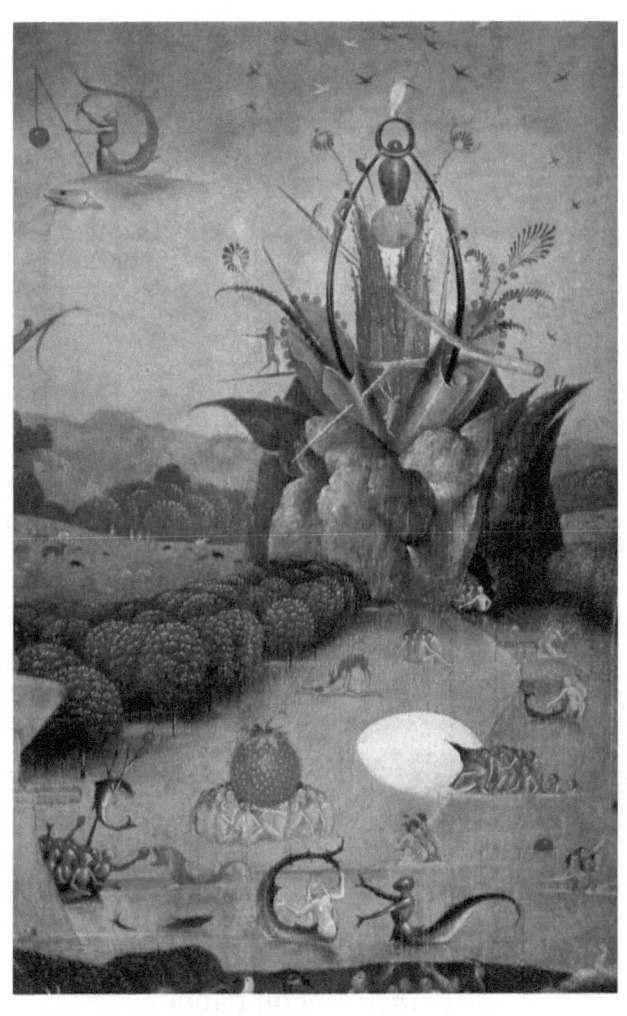

Triptych of Garden of Earthly Delights (detail)
c. 1500, Oil on panel
The picture shows a detail of the central panel,
representing the Fountain of Life with Female Rock.

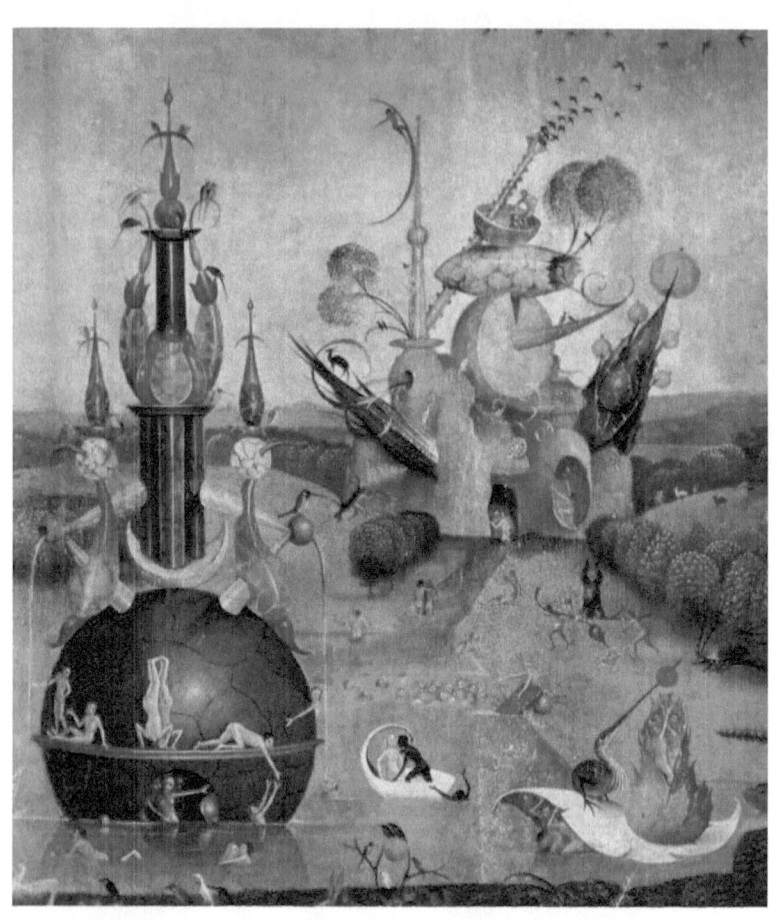

Triptych of Garden of Earthly Delights (detail)
c. 1500, Oil on panel
The picture shows a detail of the central panel,
representing the Fountain of Life with Male Rock.

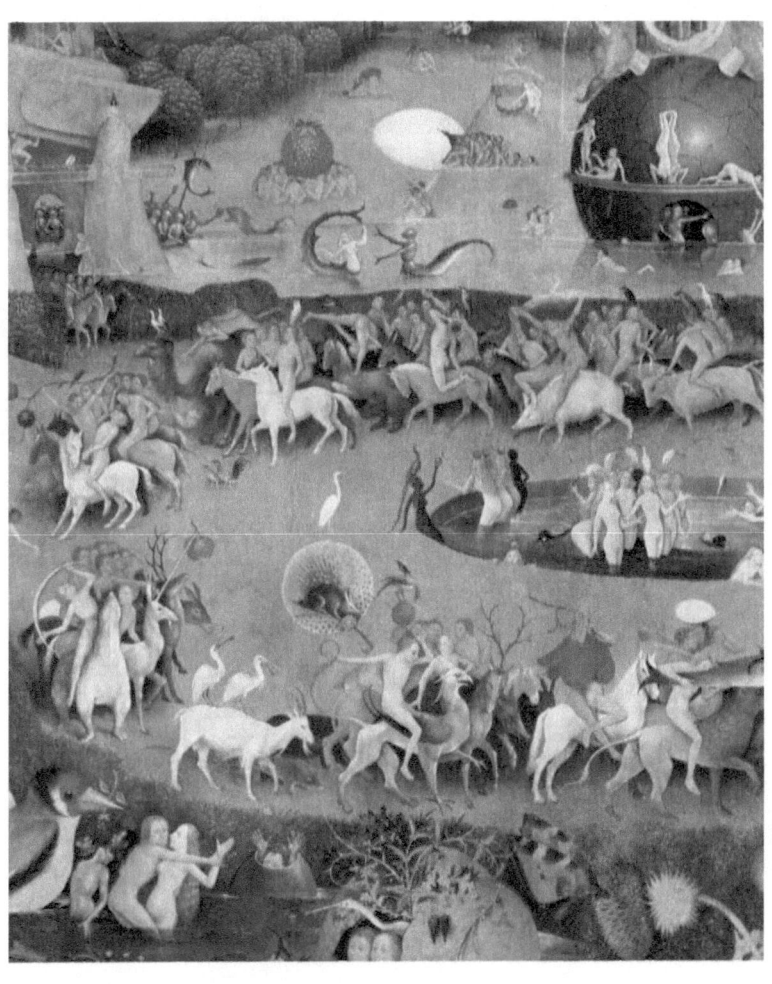

Triptych of Garden of Earthly Delights (detail)
c. 1500, Oil on panel

The picture shows a detail of the central panel, representing the Triumphal Procession around the Water of Life. The background lake is given over to mix bathing, but in the middle section the sexes are carefully segregated. The circular pool is occupied only by women, while the men ride around it on the backs of animals of different species. The antics of the acrobatic riders, one somersaulting on the back of his mount, suggest that they are excited by the presence of the women, one of whom is already climbing out of the water. By this means, of course, Bosch shows the sexual attraction between men and women, and it is not without significance that the pool and cavalcade occupy the centre of the garden, as the source and initial stage of the activity elsewhere.

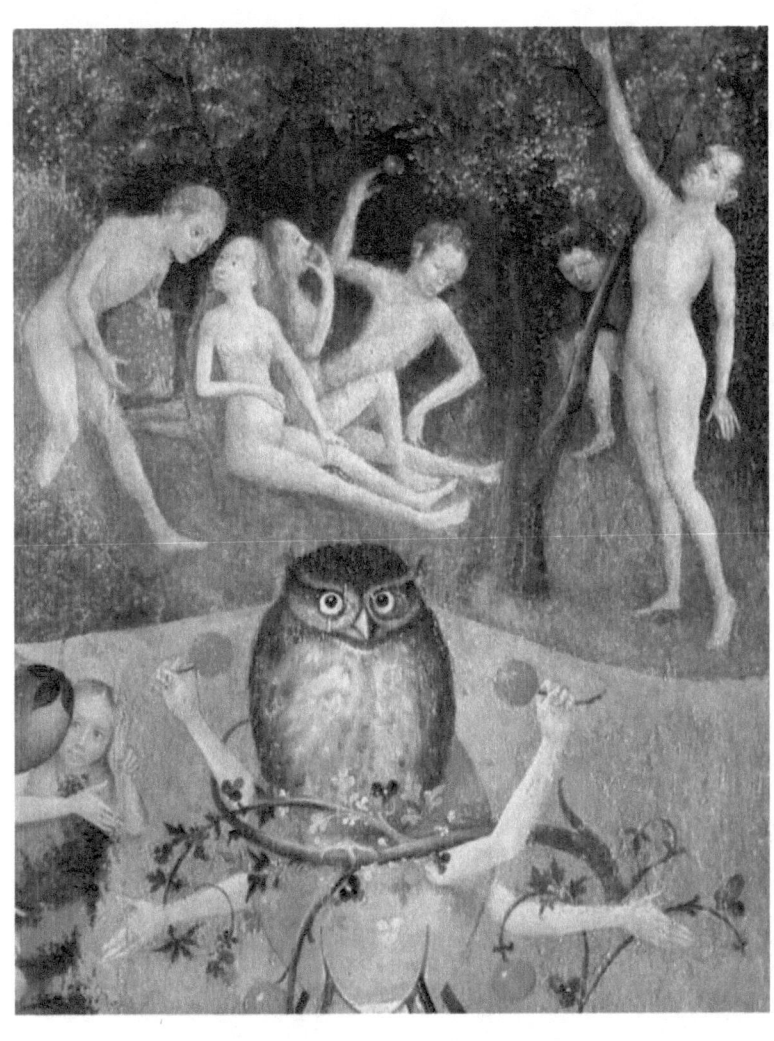

Triptych of Garden of Earthly Delights (detail)
c. 1500, Oil on panel

The picture shows a detail of the central panel, representing the Orange Grove. Scholars of Dutch literature identified many of the forms in the central panel - fruit, animals, the exotic mineral structures in the background - as erotic symbols inspired by the popular songs, sayings and slang expressions of Bosch's time. For example: many of the fruits nibbled and held by the lovers in the garden serve as metaphors of the sexual organs. The group of youths and maidens picking fruit in the right middleground also possesses erotic connotations: "to pluck fruit" (or flowers) was a euphemism for the sexual act.

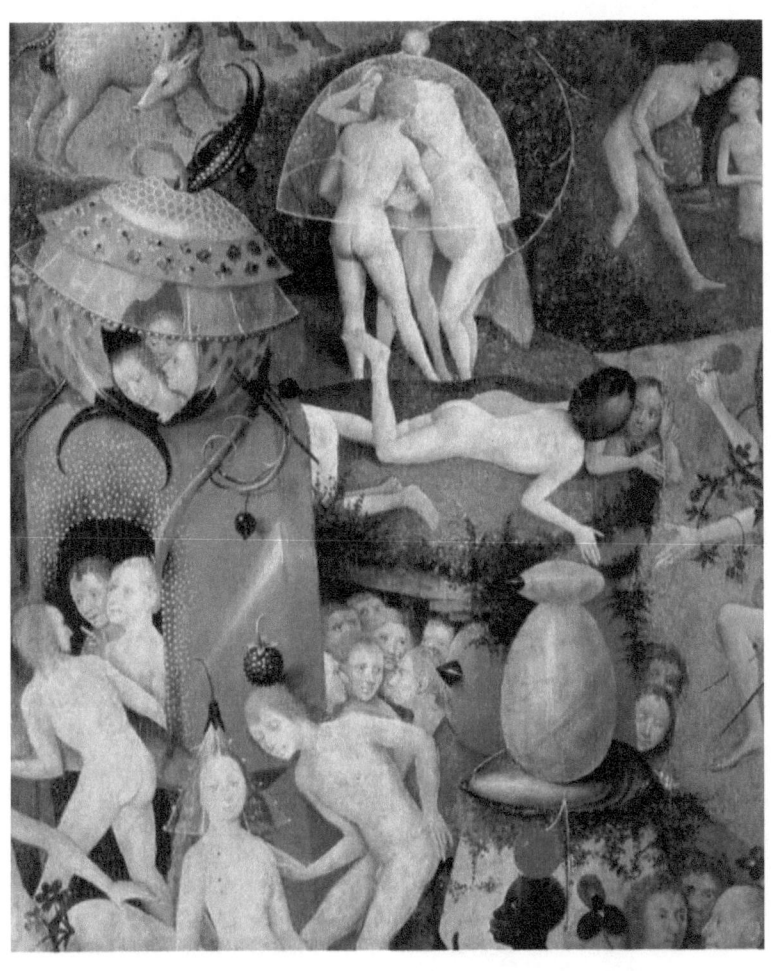

Triptych of Garden of Earthly Delights (detail)
c. 1500, Oil on panel
The picture shows a detail of the central panel,
representing the Gate to the Paradise.

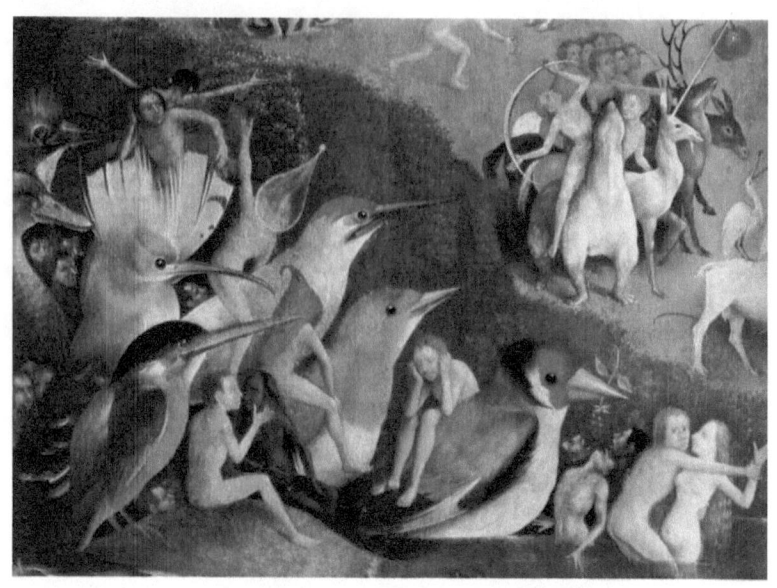

Triptych of Garden of Earthly Delights (detail)
c. 1500, Oil on panel

The picture shows a detail of the central panel,
representing the Bird Wedding.

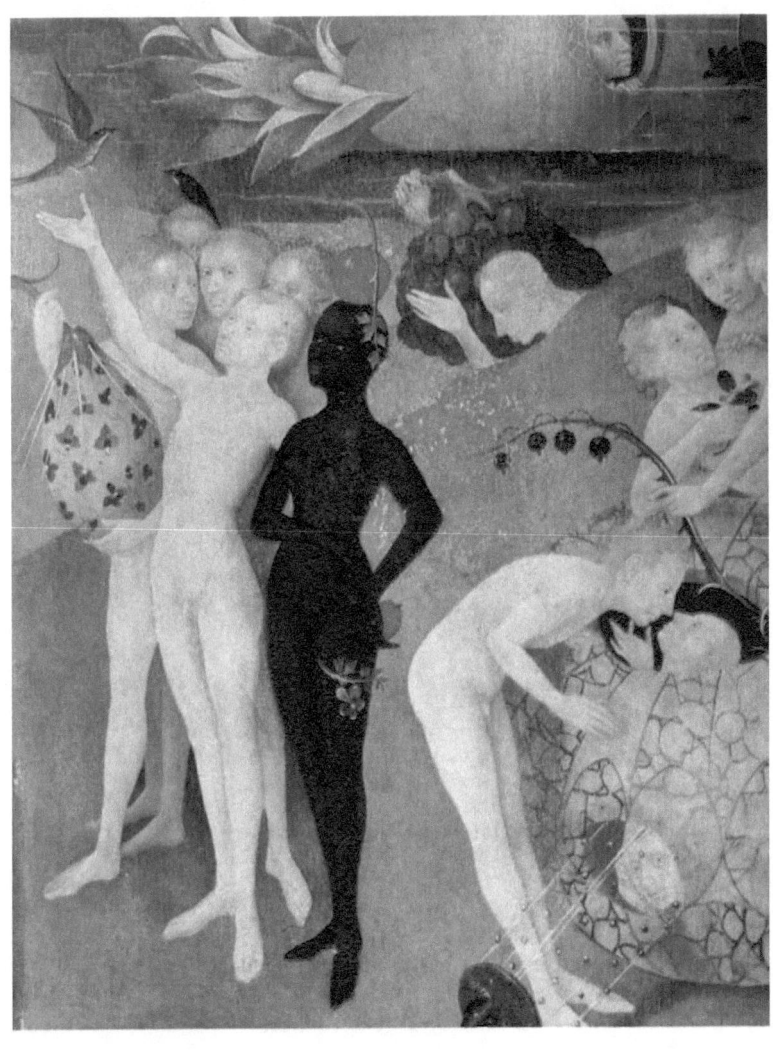

Triptych of Garden of Earthly Delights (detail)
c. 1500, Oil on panel

The picture shows a detail of the central panel,
representing the Eulogy of Virility.

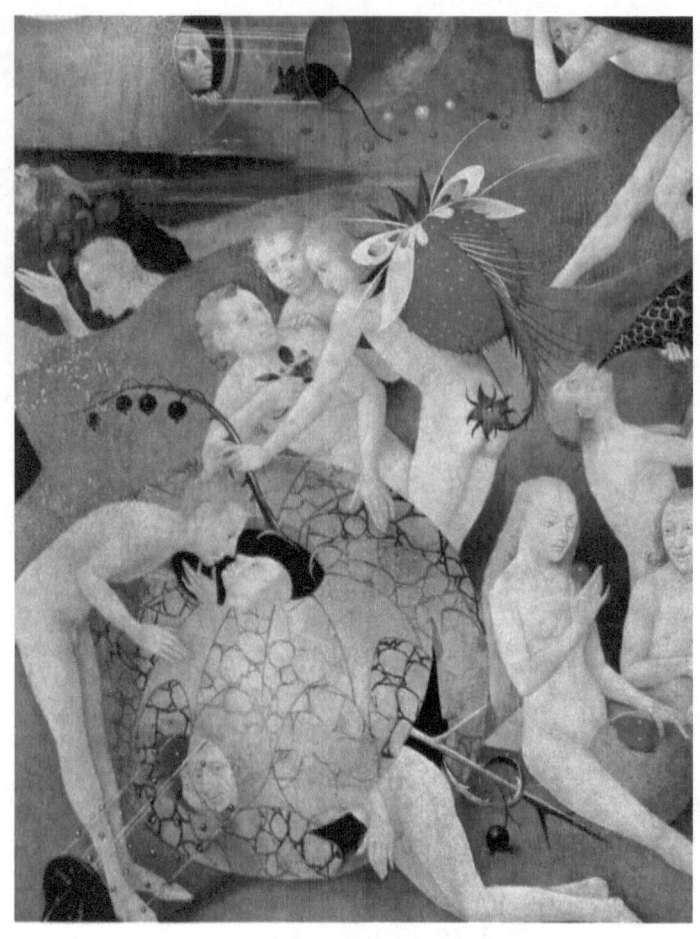

Triptych of Garden of Earthly Delights (detail)
c. 1500, Oil on panel

The picture shows a detail of the central panel,
representing the Bridal Chamber in Pumpkin. Along
with the fairly obvious representations, however, the
carnal life is also alluded to in metaphorical or
symbolic terms. The strawberries which figure so
prominently in the landscape, for instance, probably
symbolize the unsubstantial quality of fleshly pleasure.

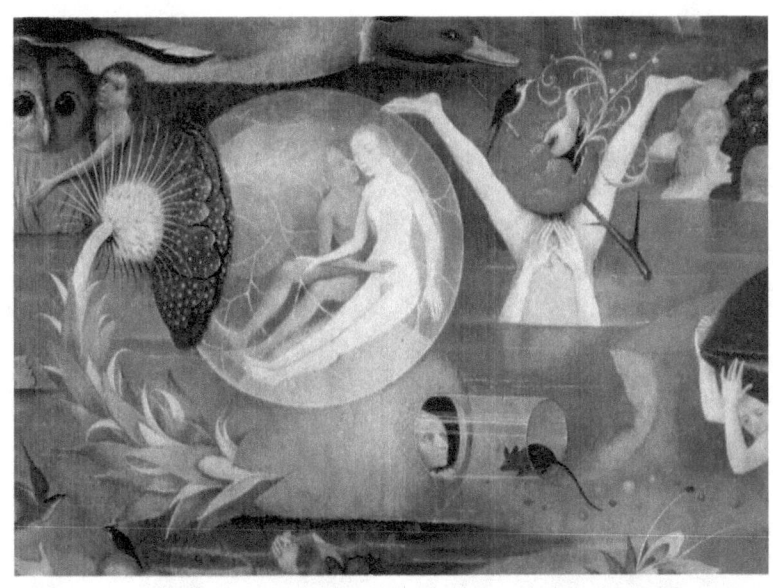

Triptych of Garden of Earthly Delights (detail)
c. 1500, Oil on panel

The picture shows a detail of the central panel, representing the Bridal Chamber in Semen Capsule.Various aspects of the deadly sin Lust are acted out in a forthright fashion, for example, by the couple enclosed in a bubble at the lower left, other figures seem to display perverted acts of love, such as the man plunged head first into the water and shielding his privy parts with his hands.

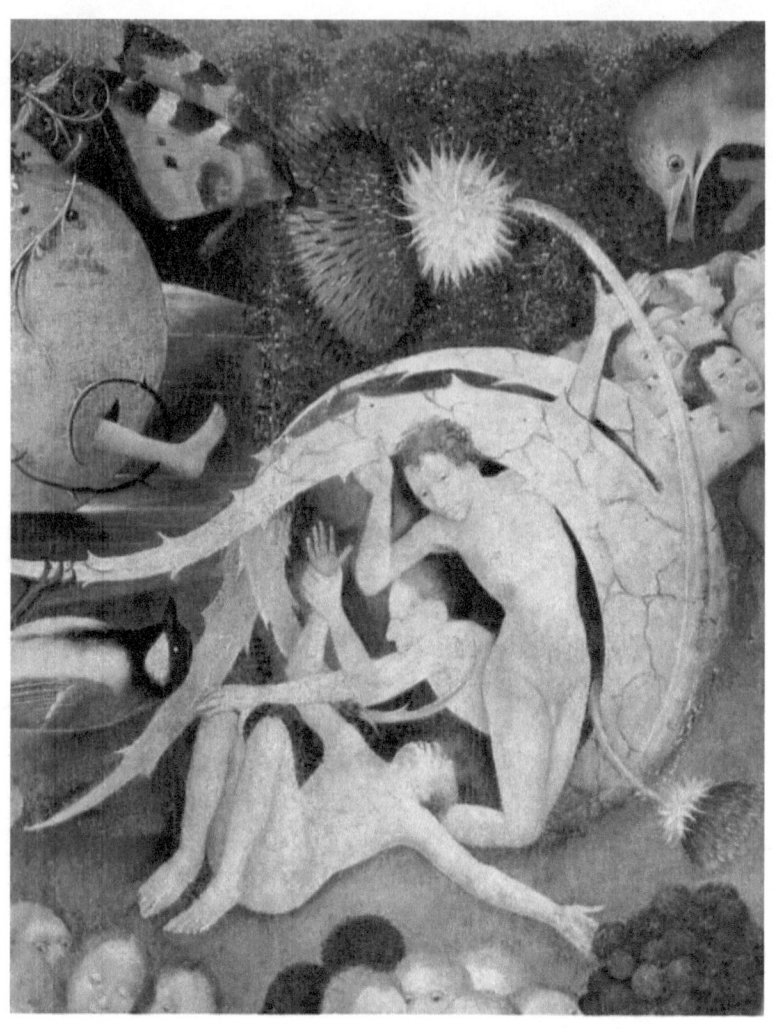

Triptych of Garden of Earthly Delights (detail)
c. 1500, Oil on panel
The picture shows a detail of the central panel,
representing the Death Thistle.

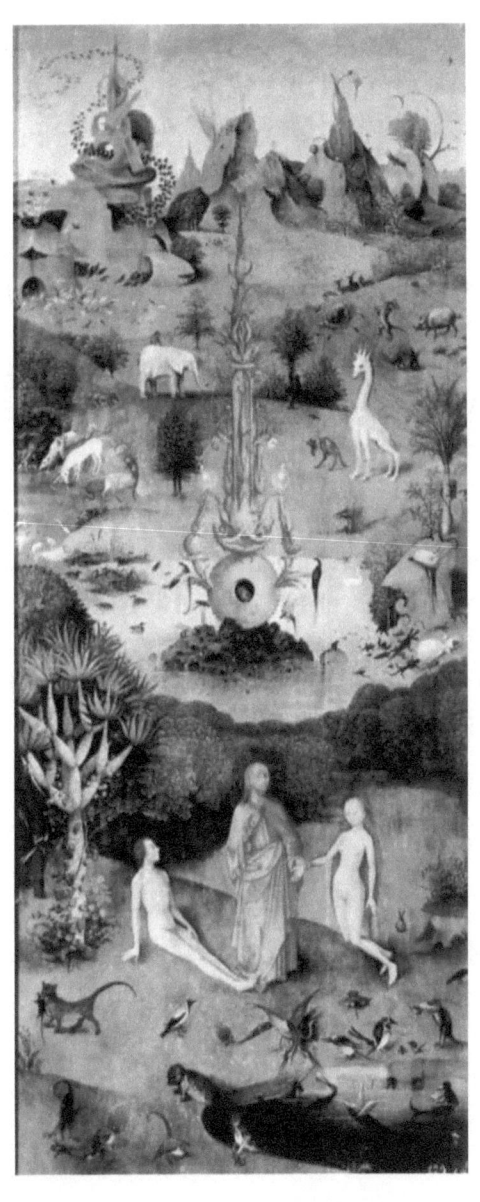

Triptych of Garden of Earthly Delights (left wing)
c. 1500, Oil on panel, 220 x 97 cm

On the left wing the last three days of Creation are accomplished. The earth and water have brought forth their swarms of living creatures, including a giraffe, an elephant, and some wholly fabulous animals, like the unicorn. In the centre rises the Fountain of Life, a tall, slender roseate structure resembling a delicately carved Gothic tabernacle. The precious gems glittering in the mud at its base and some of the more fanciful animals probably reflect the medieval descriptions of India, whose marvels had fascinated the West since the days of Alexander the Great and where popular belief situated the lost Paradise of Eden.

 In the foreground of this antediluvian landscape, we see the union of Adam and Eve by Christ. Taking Eve by the hand, he presents her to the newly awakened Adam who gazes at this creation from his rib with a mixture of surprise and anticipation.

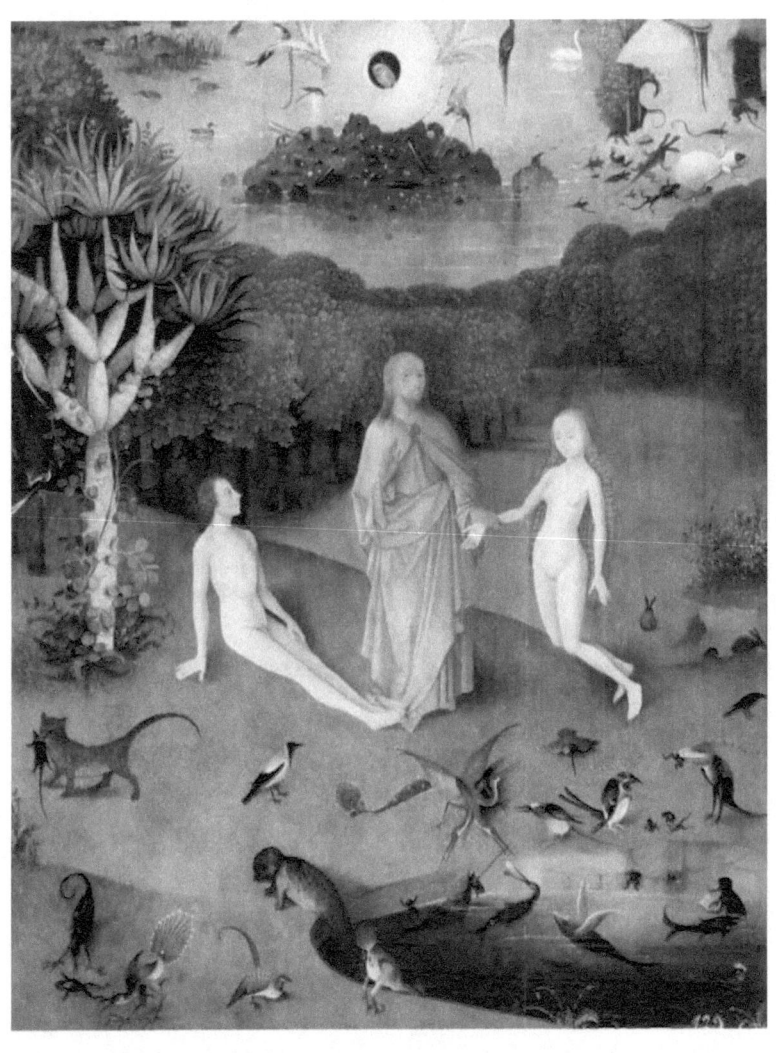

Triptych of Garden of Earthly Delights (detail)
c. 1500, Oil on panel

The picture shows a detail of the left wing, representing
Christ with Adam and Eve. Taking Eve by the hand,
God presents her to the newly awakened Adam who
gazes at this creation from his rib with a mixture, it
seems, of surprise and anticipation.

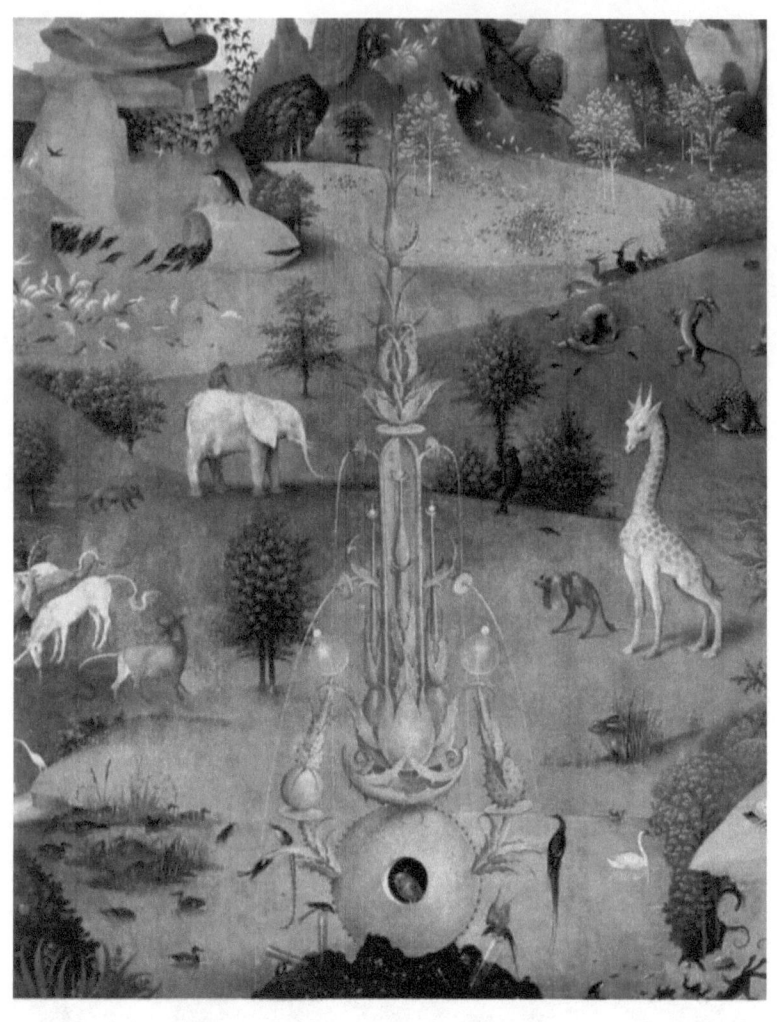

Triptych of Garden of Earthly Delights (detail)
c. 1500, Oil on panel
The picture shows a detail of the left wing, representing
the Fountain of Life.

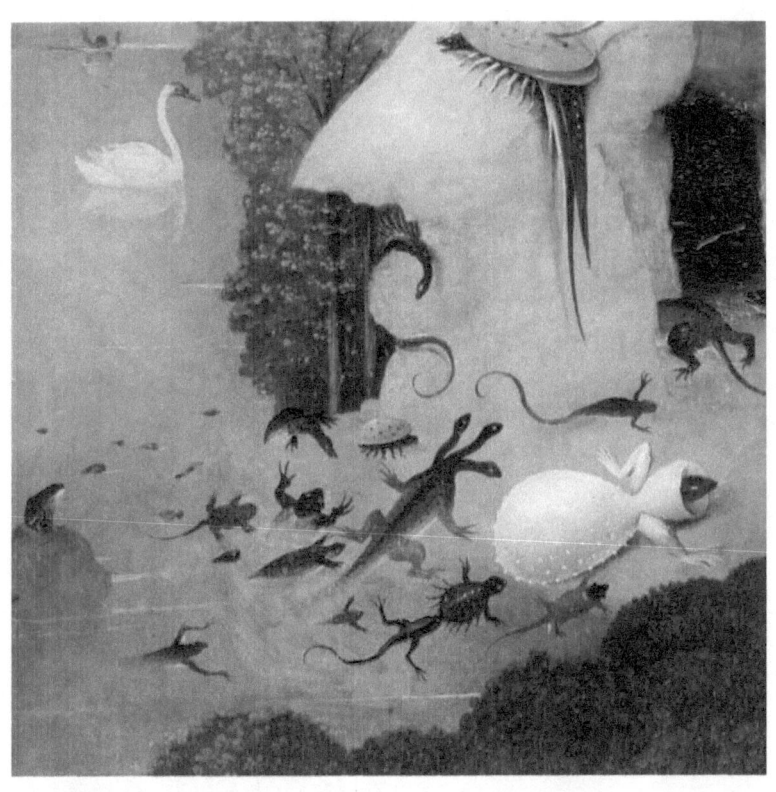

Triptych of Garden of Earthly Delights (detail)
c. 1500, Oil on panel
The picture shows a detail of the left wing, representing
the Salamander.

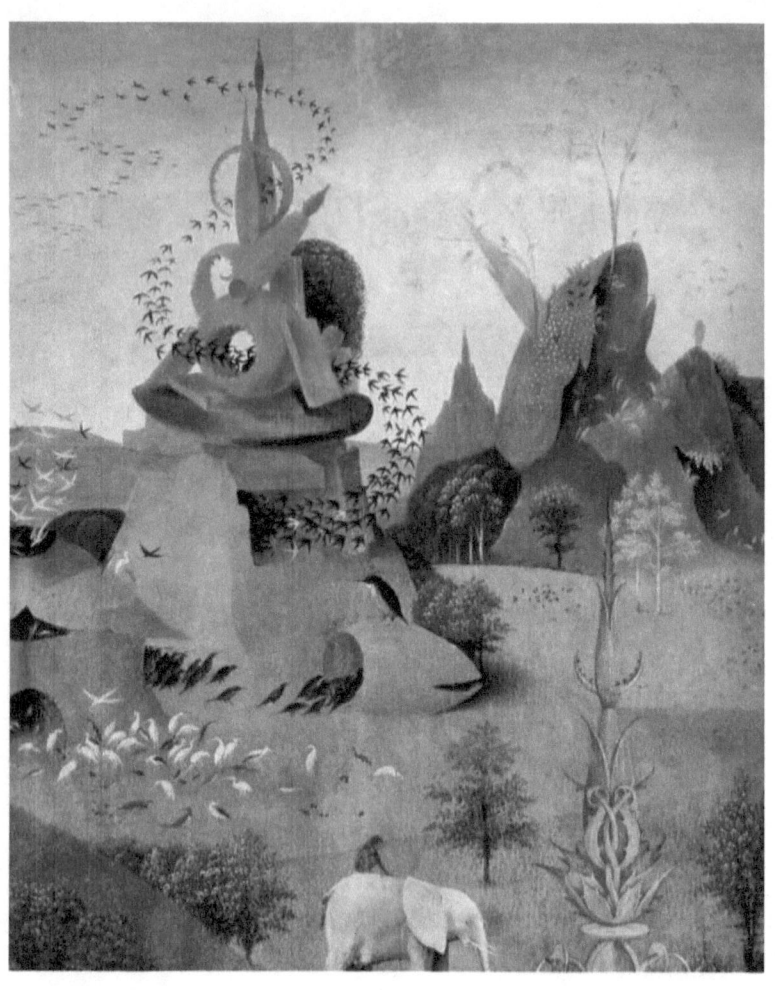

Triptych of Garden of Earthly Delights (detail)
c. 1500, Oil on panel
The picture shows a detail of the left wing, representing
the Bird Rock.

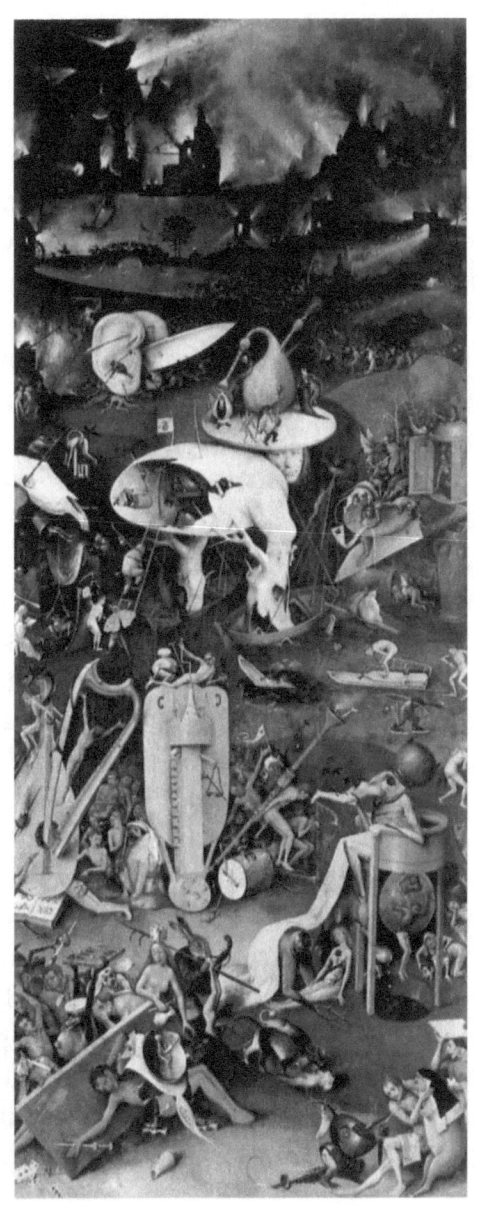

Triptych of Garden of Earthly Delights (right wing)
c. 1500, Oil on panel, 220 x 97 cm

The erotic dream of the garden of delights gives way to the nightmare reality of the right wing. It is Bosch's most violent vision of Hell. Buildings do not simply burn, they explode into the murky background, their fiery reflections turning the water below into blood. In the foreground a rabbit carries his bleeding victim on a pole, a motif found elsewhere in Bosch's Hell scenes, but this time the blood spurts forth from the belly as if propelled by gunpowder. The hunted-become-hunter well expresses the chaos of Hell, where the normal relationships of the world are turned upside down. This is even more dramatically conveyed in the innocuous everyday objects which have swollen to monstrous proportions and serve as instruments of torture; they are comparable to the oversized fruits and birds of the central panel. One nude figure is attached by devils to the neck of a lute; another is helplessly entangled in the strings of a harp, while a third soul has been stuffed down the neck of a great horn. On the frozen lake in the middle ground, a man balances uncertainly on an oversized skate, and heads straight for the hole in the ice before him, where a companion already struggles in the freezing water. Somewhat above, a group of victims have been thrust into a burning lantern which will consume them like moths, while on the opposite side, another soul dangles through the handle of a door key. Behind, a huge pair of ears advances like some infernal army tank, immolating its victims by means of a great knife.

The focal point of Hell, occupying a position analogous to that of the Fountain of Life in the Eden wing, is the so-called Tree-Man, whose egg-shaped torso rests on a pair of rotting tree trunks that end in boats for shoes. His hind quarters have fallen away, revealing a hellish tavern scene within, while his head supports a large disc on which devils and their victims promenade around a large bagpipe. The face looks over one shoulder to regard, half wistfully, the dissolution of his own body. The meaning of this enigmatic, even tragic figure has yet to be explained satisfactorily, but Bosch never created another image that more successfully evoked the shifting, insubstantial quality of a dream.

Much more solid, in contrast, is the bird-headed monster at lower right, who gobbles up the damned souls only to defecate them into a transparent chamber pot from which they plunge into a pit below. Other sins can be identified in the area around the pit. The slothful man is visited in his bed by demons, and the glutton is forced to disgorge his food, while the proud lady is compelled to admire her charms reflected in the backside of a devil. The knight brought down by a pack of hounds to the right of the Tree-Man is most likely guilty of the sin of Anger, and perhaps also of Sacrilege, for he clutches a chalice in one mailed fist. The tumultuous group at right suffers for the excesses associated with gambling and taverns.

Lust is punished in the lower right-hand corner, where an amorous sow tries to persuade her companion to sign the legal document in his lap. Perhaps he is a monk, for the sow wears the headdress of a nun. An armoured monster waits near by with an inkwell dangling from his beak. Lust is also the subject of the oversized musical instruments and choral singing in the left foreground. The musical instruments themselves often possessed erotic connotations. The bagpipe also figured as an emblem of the male organ of generation, while to play the lute signified making love.

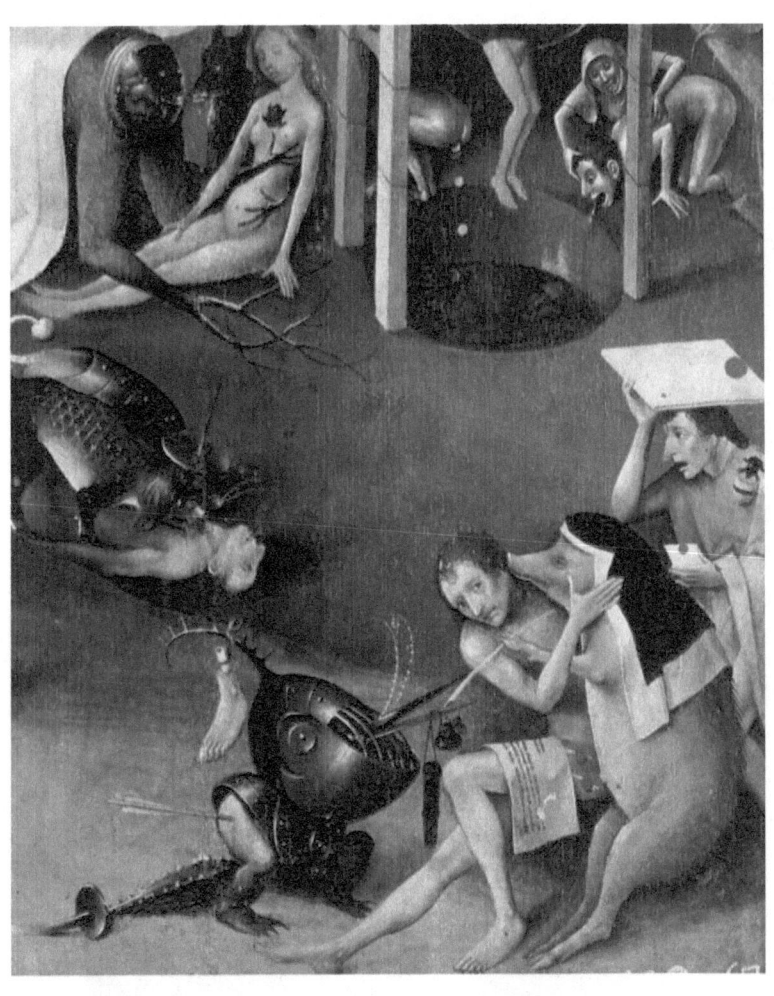

Triptych of Garden of Earthly Delights (detail)
c. 1500, Oil on panel

The detail represents the Legacy Hunter. Lust is punished in the lower right-hand corner, where an amorous sow tries to persuade her companion to sign the legal document in his lap. Perhaps he is a monk, for the sow wears the headdress of a nun. An armoured monster waits near by with an inkwell dangling from his beak.

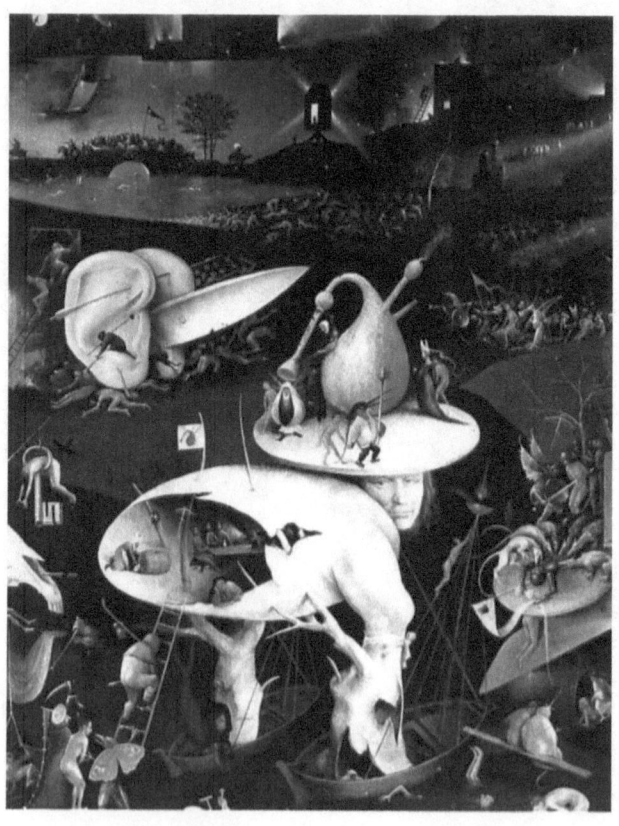

Triptych of Garden of Earthly Delights (detail)
c. 1500, Oil on panel
The picture shows a detail of the right wing.

The focal point of Hell is the so-called Tree-Man, whose egg-shaped torso rests on a pair of rotting tree trunks that end in boats for shoes. His hind quarters have fallen away, revealing a hellish tavern scene within, while his head supports a large disc on which devils and their victims promenade around a large bagpipe. The face looks over one shoulder to regard, half wistfully, the dissolution of his own body. The meaning of this enigmatic, even tragic figure has yet to be explained satisfactorily, but Bosch never created another image that more successfully evoked the shifting, insubstantial quality of a dream.

Behind a huge pair of ears advances like some infernal army tank, immolating its victims by means of a great knife. The letter M engraved on the knife, which also appears on other knives in Bosch's paintings, has been thought to represent the hallmark of some cutler whom the artist particularly disliked, but it more likely refers to 'Mundus' (World), or possibly Antichrist, whose name, according to some medieval prophecies, would begin with this letter.

The knight brought down by a pack of hounds to the right of the Tree-Man is most likely guilty of the sin of Anger, and perhaps also of Sacrilege, for he clutches a chalice in one mailed fist.

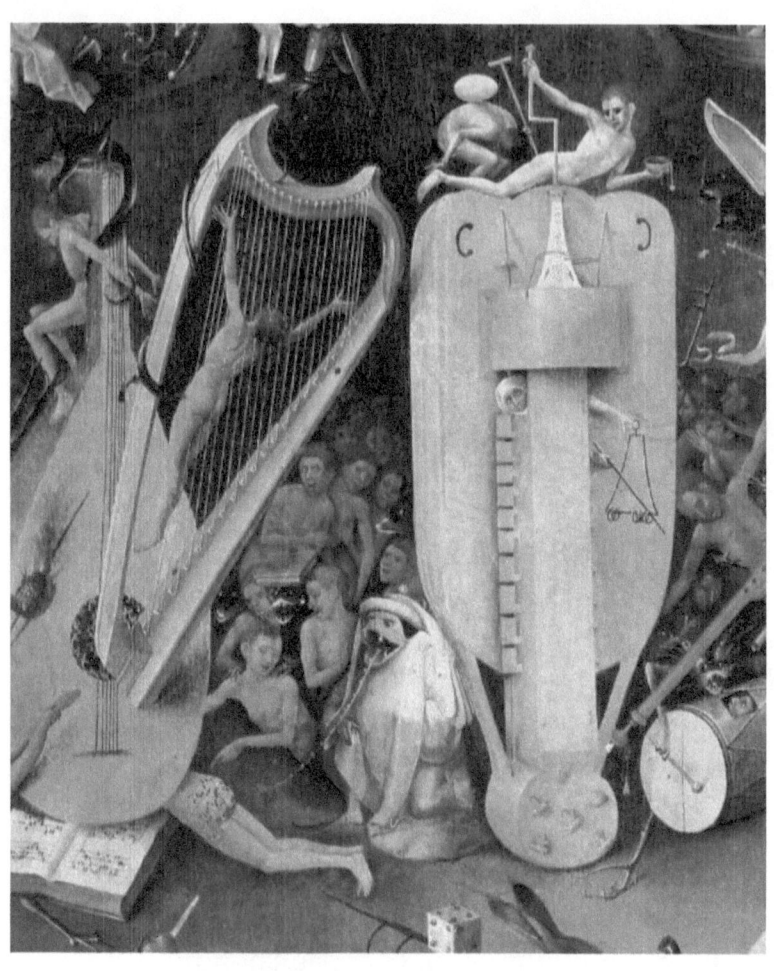

Triptych of Garden of Earthly Delights (detail)
c. 1500, Oil on panel
The picture shows a detail of the right wing which
represents the Musicians' Level.

In the Hell the normal relationships of the world are turned upside down. This is dramatically conveyed in the innocuous everyday objects which have swollen to monstrous proportions and serve as instruments of torture. One nude figure is attached by devils to the neck of a lute; another is helplessly entangled in the strings of a harp.

Several huge musical instruments figure prominently in Bosch's conception of hell. They are shaped similarly to the ones used at that time, but their positioning is unrealistic (for example, a harp grows out of a lute). Their relationship to each other bears strongly fanciful elements, and they have been adapted in form. What is more, the use of these instruments is wholly fantastic. There is a human figure stretched across the strings of a harp; another writhes around the neck of a flute, intertwined with a snake; a third peers out of a drum equipped with bird-like feet, the next one plays triangle while reaching out from a hurdy-gurdy, and even the smoking trumpet displays an outstretched human arm. It is difficult to conceive that the group of damned souls would sing a hymn from the musical score fixed to the reverse of the reclining figure in front of them - although this has been proposed by some scholars. The ensemble, lead by an infernal monster, could more likely be a parody.

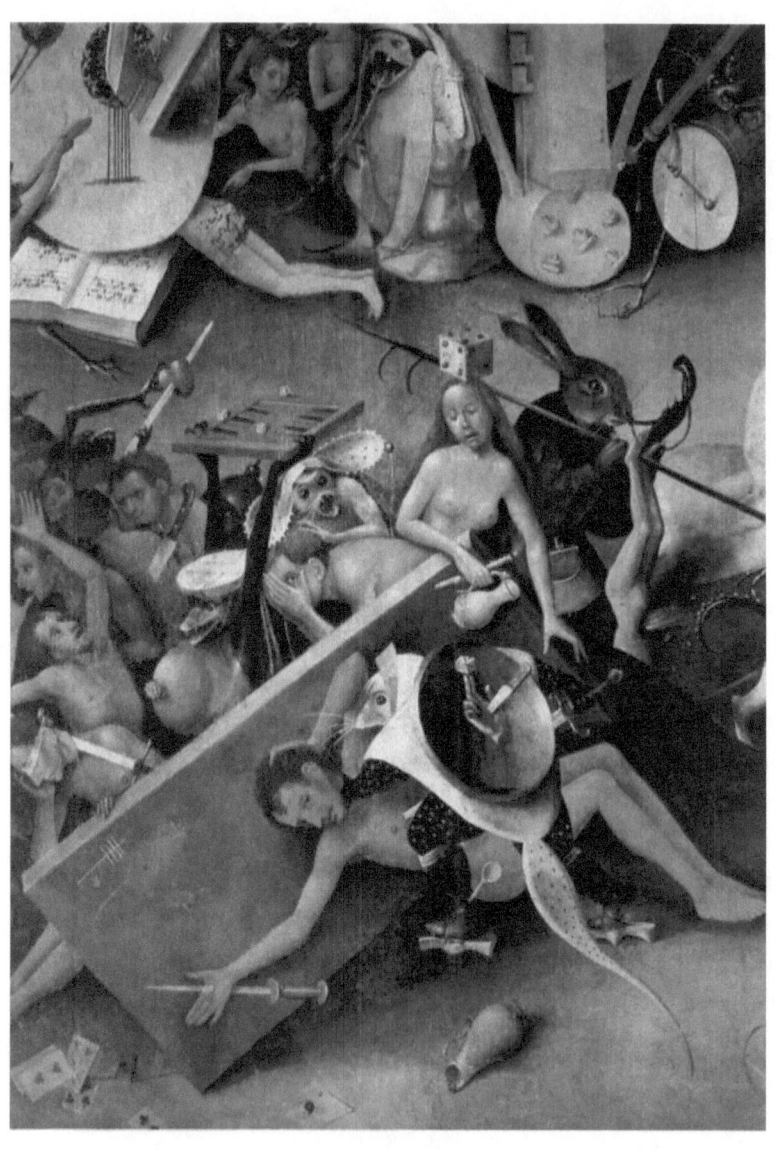

Triptych of Garden of Earthly Delights (detail)
c. 1500, Oil on panel

The picture shows a detail of the right wing which represents the Gamblers' Level. The tumultuous group at right suffers for the excesses associated with gambling and taverns. Behinf them a rabbit carries his bleeding victim on a pole, a motif found elsewhere in Bosch's Hell scenes, but this time the blood spurts forth from the belly as if propelled by gunpowder. The hunted-become-hunter well expresses the chaos of Hell, where the normal relationships of the world are turned upside down.

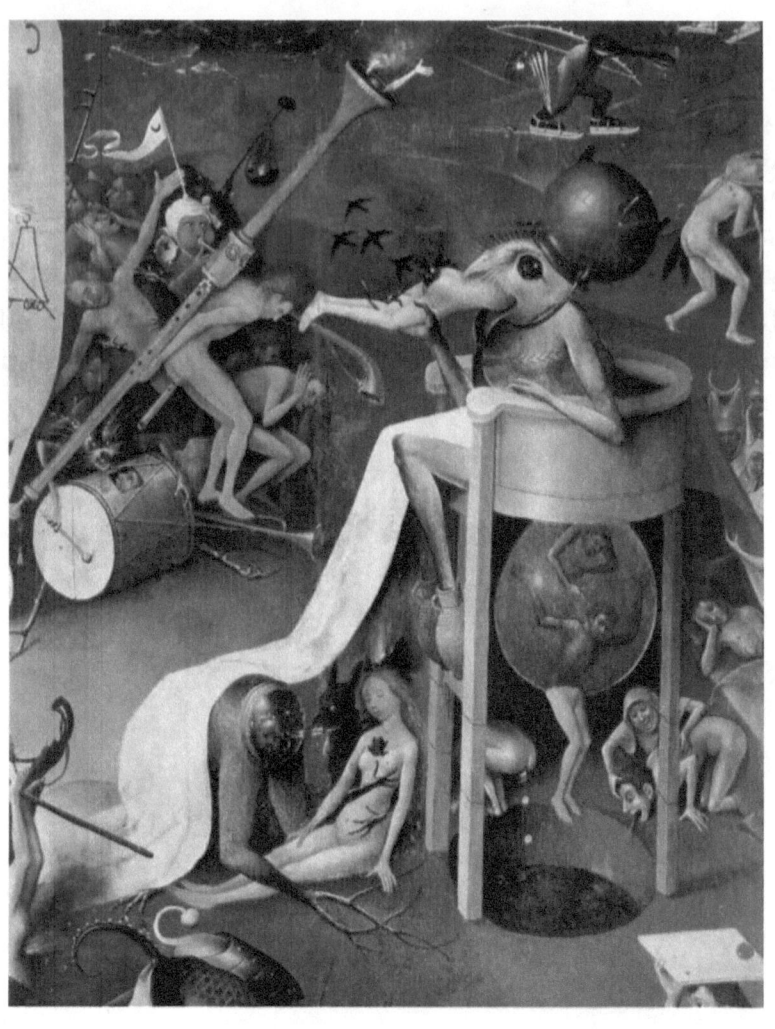

Triptych of Garden of Earthly Delights (detail)
c. 1500, Oil on panel

The picture shows a detail of the right wing which represents the bird-headed monster. The bird-headed monster at lower right gobbles up the damned souls only to defecate them into a transparent chamber pot from which they plunge into a pit below. Other sins can be identified in the area around the pit. The slothful man is visited in his bed by demons, and the glutton is forced to disgorge his food, while the proud lady is compelled to admire her charms reflected in the backside of a devil.

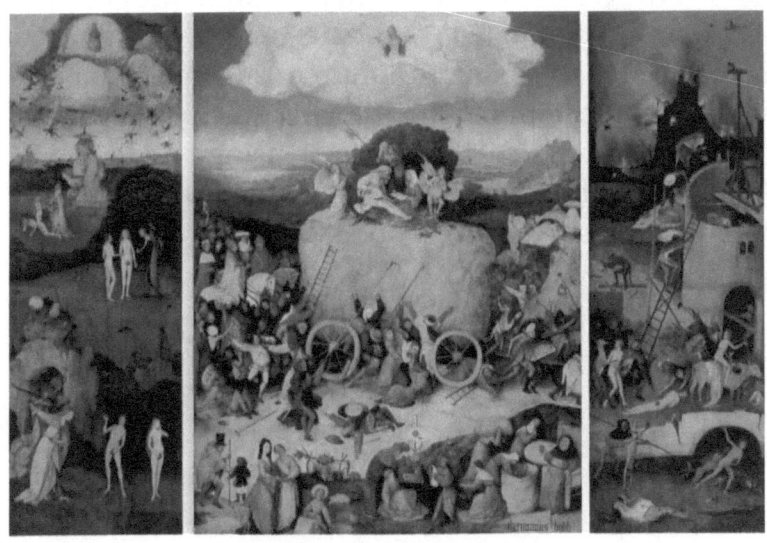

Triptych of Haywain
1500-02, Oil on panel, 135 x 190 cm

The Haywain triptych exists in two versions, one in the Escorial, the other in the Prado, Madrid. Both are in poor condition and have been heavily restored, and scholars disagree as to which is the original. The left inner wing presents the Creation and Fall of Man, and the expulsion of the rebel angels, the right wing is occupied by a view of Hell. The central panel presents a new image: a curious vehicle, a great haywain lumbering across a vast landscape, being pulled by devils towards Hell and damnation. The subject of sin and its punishments was central to all of Bosch's art. A famous triptych, The Haywain, contains a progression of sin, from Eden to hell, across its panels. In the central panel sin is represented through the metaphor of a large wagonload of hay for which a greedy world grasps. All the while, the wagon is being pulled by demons towards the right panel - which shows one of Bosch's earliest depictions of hell.

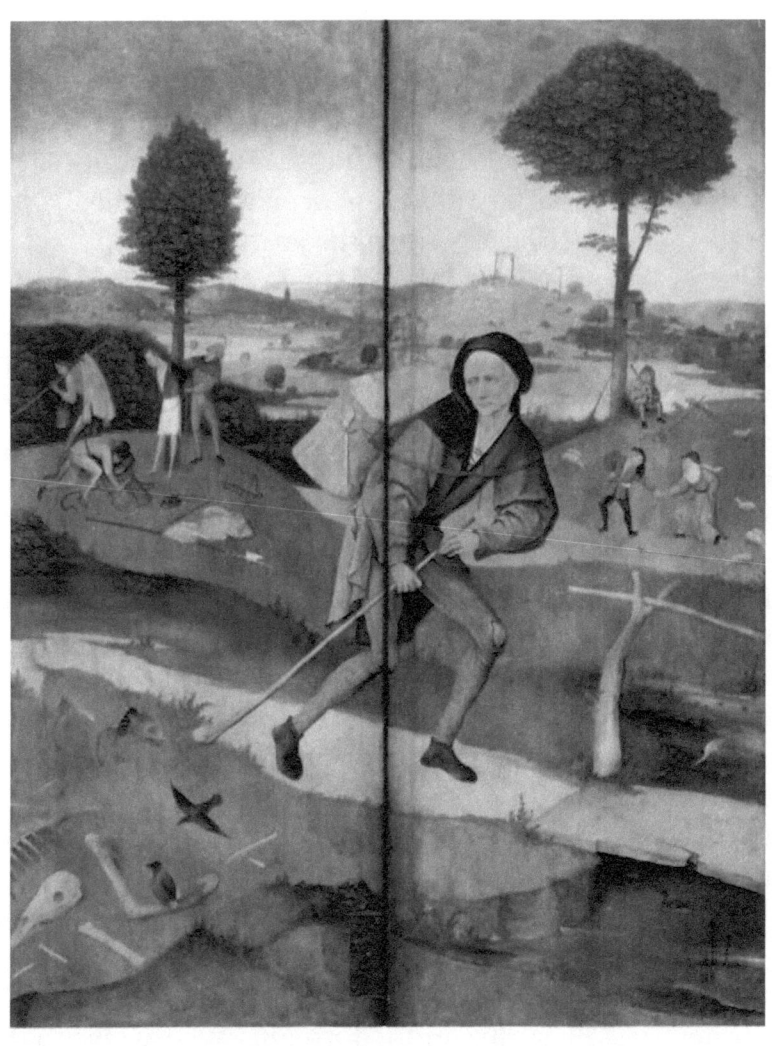

Triptych of Haywain (outer wings)
1500-02, Oil on panel, 135 x 90 cm

The scene on the outer wings of the Haywain triptych is called Wayfarer or the Path of Life.

The foreground is dominated by an emaciated, shabbily dressed man who is no longer young, carrying a wicker basket strapped to his back; he travels through a menacing landscape. A skull and several bones lie scattered at lower left; an ugly cur snaps at his heels, while the footbridge on which he is about to step appears very fragile indeed. In the background, bandits have robbed another traveller and are binding him to a tree, and peasants dance at the right to the skirl of a bagpipe. A crowd of people gather around an enormous gallows in the distance, not far from a tall pole surmounted by a wheel, used for displaying the bodies of executed criminals.

Bosch's pilgrim makes his way through the treacherous world whose vicissitudes are represented in the landscape. Some of the dangers are physical, such as the robbers or the snarling dog, although the latter may also symbolize detractors and slanderers, whose evil tongues were often compared to barking dogs. The dancing peasants, however, connote a moral danger; like the lovers on top of the haywain, they have succumbed to the music of the flesh. In expressing the spiritual predicament of all mankind, the pilgrim thus resembles Everyman and his Dutch and German counterparts Elckerlijc and Jedermann, whose spiritual pilgrimages form the subjects of contemporary morality plays.

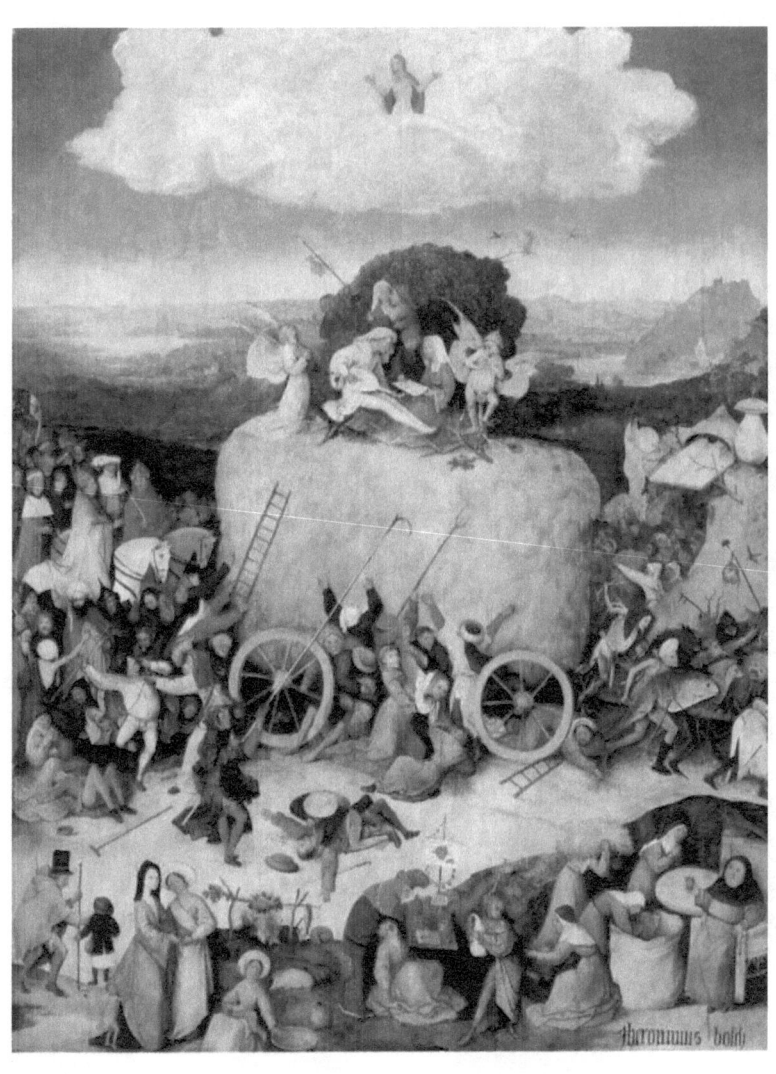

Triptych of Haywain (central panel)
1500-02, Oil on panel, 135 x 100 cm

Like the Tabletop of the Seven Deadly Sins, the Haywain shows mankind given over to sin, completely unmindful of God's law and oblivious to the fate which he has prepared for them. In this image, however, Bosch focuses on one of the Deadly Sins: the desire for worldly gain, or Avarice, whose sub-categories are elaborated in the adjacent figure groups very much as they are in the old handbooks on the Virtues and Vices. Avarice leads to discord, violence and even murder, all of which are graphically depicted in the open space before the cart. If the princes and prelates complacently jog along behind the cart, holding themselves aloof from this struggle, it is because the haystack is, so to speak, already in their possession; they are guilty of the sin of Pride. Avarice also leads men to cheat and deceive; the man wearing a tall hat and accompanied by a child at lower left is most likely a false beggar. The quack physician in the centre has set up his table with charts and jars designed to impress his victim; the purse at his side stuffed with hay alludes to his ill-gotten gains. Several nuns at lower right push hay into a large bag, supervised by a seated monk whose gluttonous tendencies are revealed by his ample waist.

The meaning of some of the other groups remains unclear, and we may also wonder at the presence of the lovers on top of the haystack. That they illustrate the sin of Lust we know from the appearance of similar figures in the Prado Tabletop, but it might be argued that the pursuit of the pleasures of the flesh involves the expenditure rather than the accumulation of earthly goods. A class distinction may perhaps be observed between the rustic couple kissing in the bushes and the more elegantly dressed group making music. Their music is certainly that of the flesh, for the devil near by, piping some lascivious tune through his nose, has already lured their attention from the angel praying at the left.

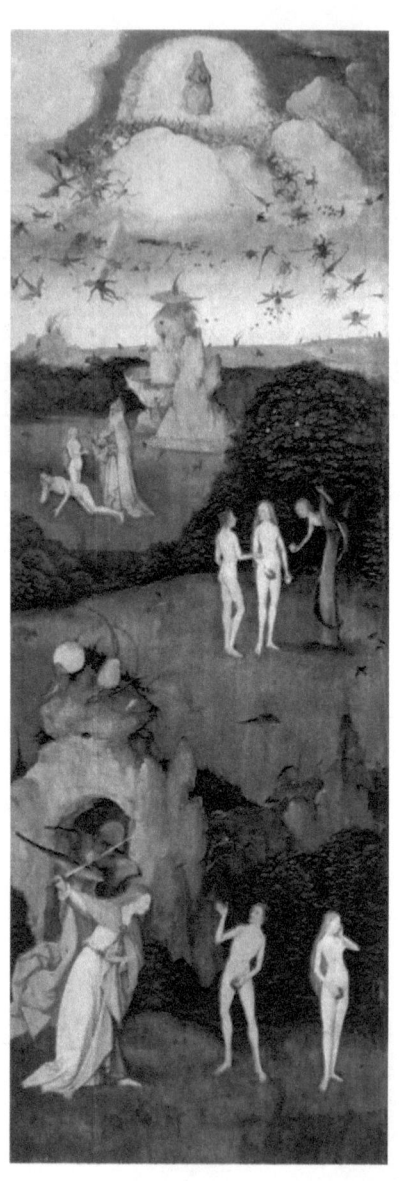

Triptych of Haywain (left wing)
1500-02, Oil on panel, 135 x 45 cm

The left wing of the triptych represents the Paradise. As in the Last Judgment, the left inner wing presents the Creation and Fall of Man (reversing, however, the sequence of episodes from foreground to background) and the expulsion of the Rebel Angels.

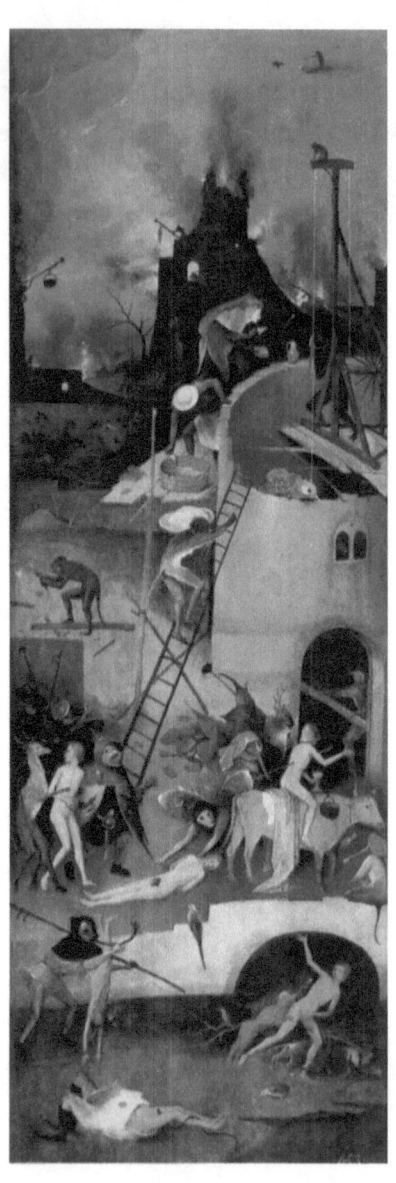

Triptych of Haywain (right wing)
1500-02, Oil on panel, 135 x 45 cm

The right wing of the triptych represents the Hell.

In composition, the Hellscape of the right wing of the Haywain stands between the discursive panorama of the Vienna Last Judgment and the monumental simplicity of the Hell panel at Venice. Reminiscent of the latter work, too, are the tall blasted ruin silhouetted against the flaming background and the damned souls struggling helplessly in the lake below, although the foreground is dominated by a new motif, a circular tower whose process of construction is shown in circumstantial detail. One demon climbs a ladder with fresh mortar for the devil masons on the scaffolding above, while a black-skinned companion raises a floor beam with a hoist.

The significance of this feverish activity is not clear. Towers abound in medieval descriptions of Hell, but the devils are usually too busy ministering to their victims to engage in such architectural enterprises. However, St Gregory reports a vision of Heaven in which houses were constructed of golden bricks, each brick representing an "almsdeed" or charitable act by someone on earth, and were intended to receive the souls of the good. Perhaps Bosch has represented the hellish counterpart of these heavenly mansions, in which avarice, and not almsdeed, supplies the stones. On the other hand, Bosch's tower may be a parody of the infamous Tower of Babel with which men sought to storm the gates of Heaven itself. In this case it would symbolize Pride, the sin which caused the fall of the Rebel Angels and which is exemplified by the worldly prince and prelate and their retinue behind the haywain.

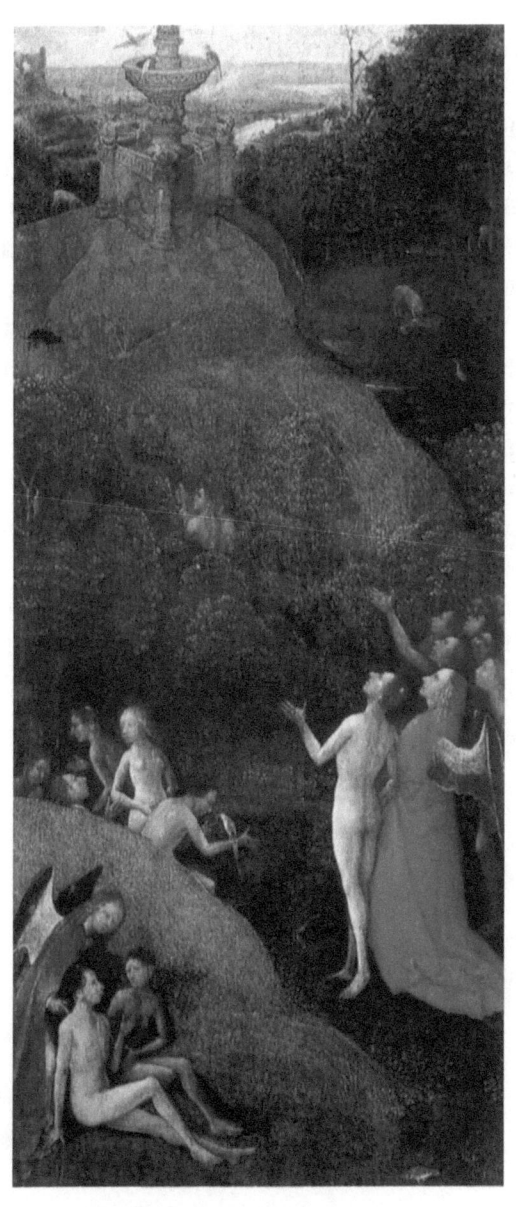

Paradise: Terrestrial Paradise
1500-04, Oil on panel, 86, 5 x 39, 5 cm

It has been assumed that the Paradise and Hell panels, inspired by a panel of Dirk Bouts, once formed the wings of a Last Judgment altarpiece; more probably, however, they were originally intended as independent works illustrating the rewards and pains of the Particular Judgment. The pictures have been disfigured by heavy overpainting and darkened varnish, and critics are not unanimous in attributing them to Bosch; nevertheless, it would be difficult to ascribe their compositions to anyone else. In the Paradise pair, the left-hand panel depicts the elect shepherded by angels into a rolling landscape from which rises the Fountain of Life; this is the Terrestrial Paradise, a sort of intermediate stage where the saved were cleansed of the last stain of sin before being admitted into the presence of God. Already one group of souls looks expectantly upwards.

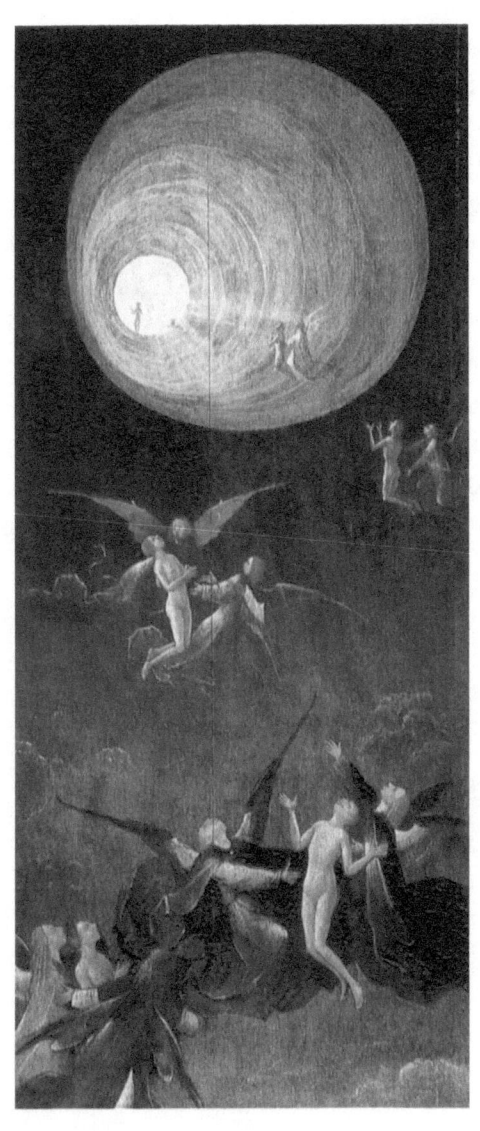

Paradise: Ascent of the Blessed
1500-04, Oil on panel, 86, 5 x 39, 5 cm

The actual entry of the saved into Heaven is depicted on a separate panel presenting a vision of celestial joy. Shedding the last vestige of their corporeality, the blessed souls float upwards through the night, scarcely supported by their angelic guides. They gaze with ecstatic yearning towards the great light which bursts through the darkness overhead. This funnel-shaped radiance, with its distinct segments, probably owes much to contemporary zodiacal diagrams, but in Bosch's hands it has become a shining corridor through which the blessed approach that final and perpetual union of the soul with God which is experienced on earth only in rare moments of spiritual exaltation.

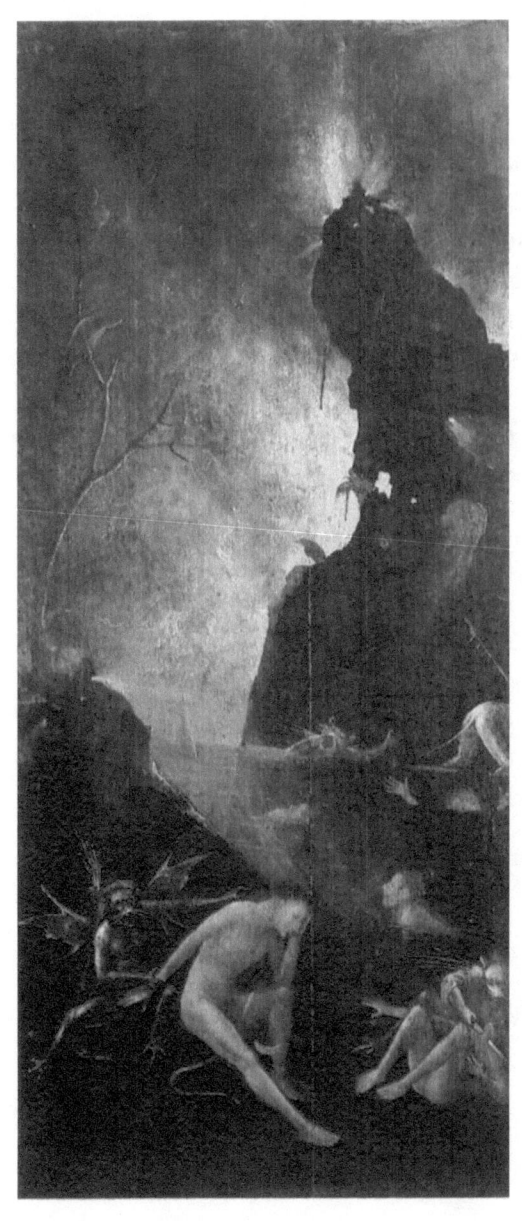

Hell
1500-04, Oil on panel, 86,5 x 39,5 cm

In the final panel, Purgatory, a craggy mountain belches forth flames against a fiery sky, while the souls struggle helplessly in the water below. Not all the torments are physical: oblivious to the bat-winged devil tugging at him, one soul sits on the shore in a pensive attitude, seemingly overwhelmed by remorse. Hell, no less than Heaven, has been interpreted in the spiritual sense of the mystics. The marked contrasts between light and shade, with sudden flashes in the sky at the top of the painting, heighten the dense and dismal atmosphere of hell, which contrasts with the serene light and colour in the two panels of paradise.

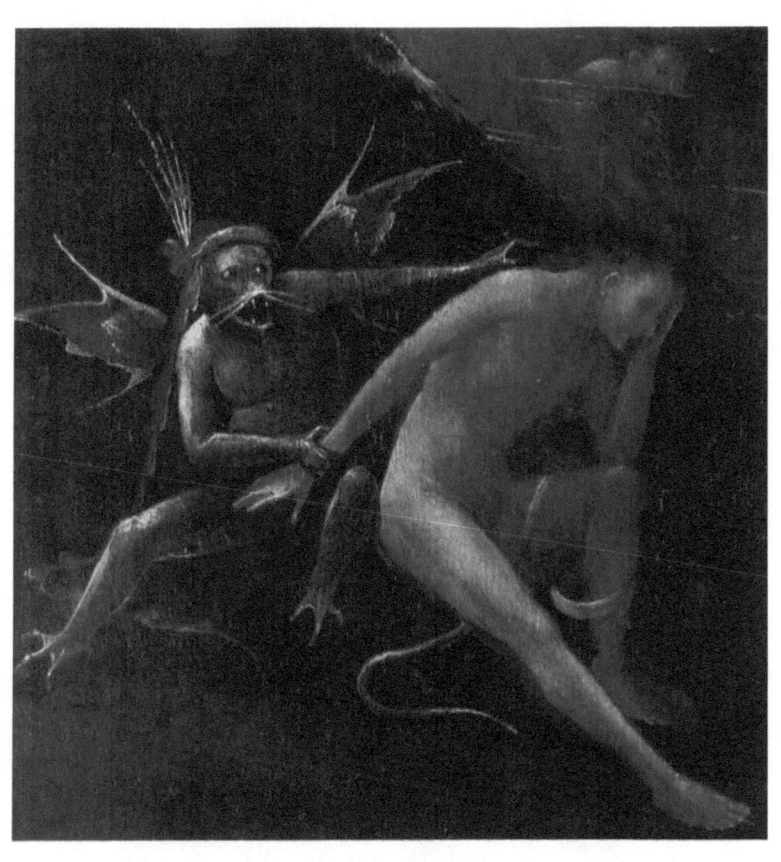

Hell (detail)
1500-04, Oil on panel, 86,5 x 39,5 cm

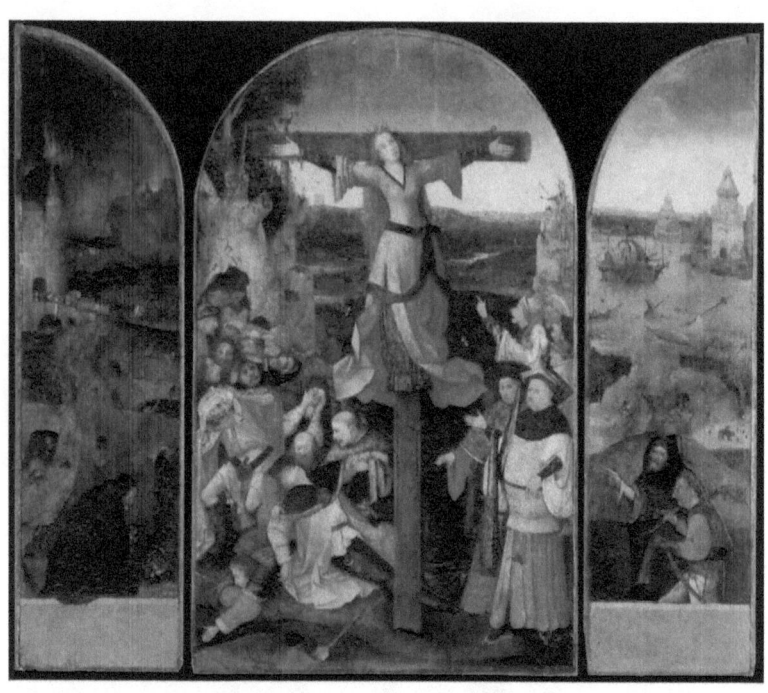

Triptych of the Martyrdom of St Liberata
1500-04, Oil on panel, 104 x 119 cm

In his pictures of the saints, Bosch seldom depicted those miraculous exploits and spectacular martyrdoms which so fascinated the later Middle Ages. The early triptych of the Crucifixion of St Liberata (Virgo fortis) is an exception. It has been proposed that Bosch painted this picture during a trip to northern Italy, but it is more likely that it was commissioned by Italian merchants or diplomats residing in the Netherlands. Earlier it was thought that the central panel represents the martyrdom of St Julia, a saint from Corsica. The attribution to Bosch of the side panels, representing St Anthony in Meditation, and Two Slave dealers, is debated.

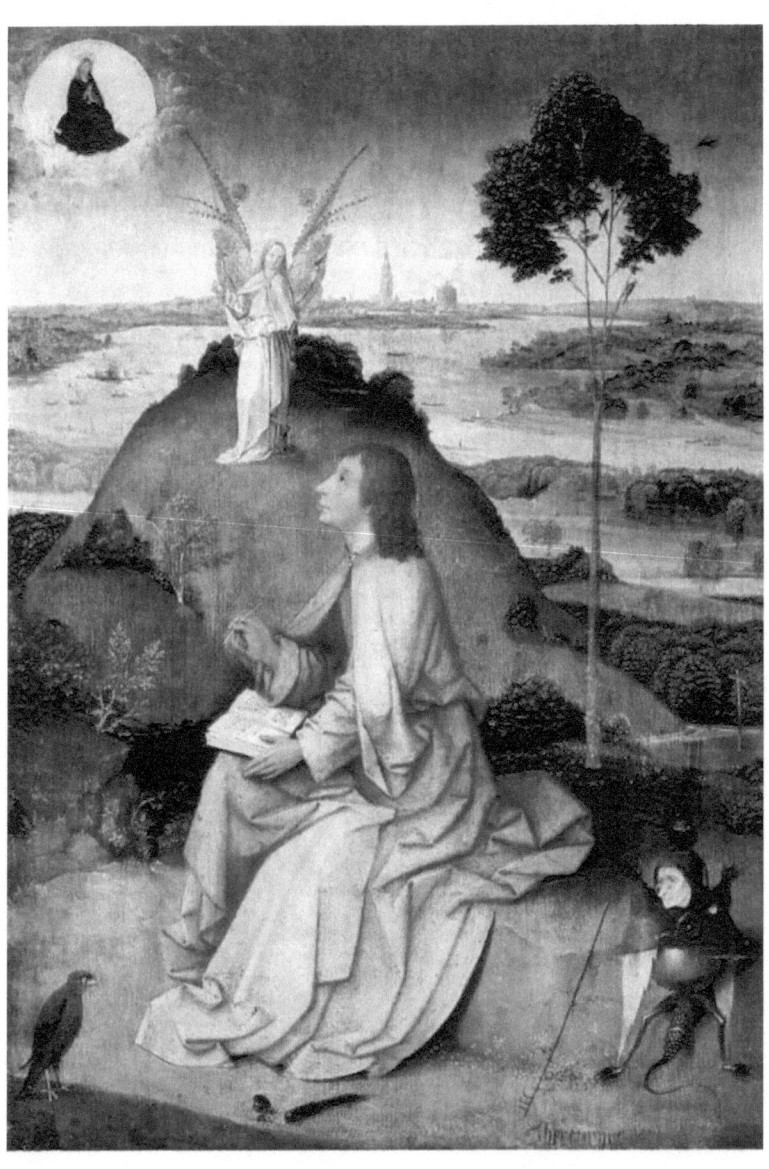

St John the Evangelist on Patmos
1504-05, Oil on oak panel, 63 x 43, 3 cm

St John the Evangelist sits on a hill in the foreground of the painting. He holds an open book in his left hand and a writing quill in his right hand. From the hill the view extends across a river landscape reminiscent of the Lower Rhine, but meant to be the island of Patmos, where John received the Revelation of the Apocalypse. An angel points towards the sky, where the Woman of the Apocalypse has appeared. Since the Middle Ages this heavenly vision has been identified with the Madonna. The bird at the bottom left is a falcon - a reference to the symbolic animal of the Evangelist, the eagle. The bird guards its master's writing tools, which a demon is trying to steal. Demons also throng the dark reverse of the panel.

Perhaps influenced by earlier representations of this subject, Bosch for once restrained his predilection for demonic spectacles. There are, to be sure, several ships burning in the water at lower left, and a little monster can be seen at lower right, both details probably suggested by St John's Apocalypse, but neither seriously disturbs the idyllic landscape in which the saint enjoys his vision.

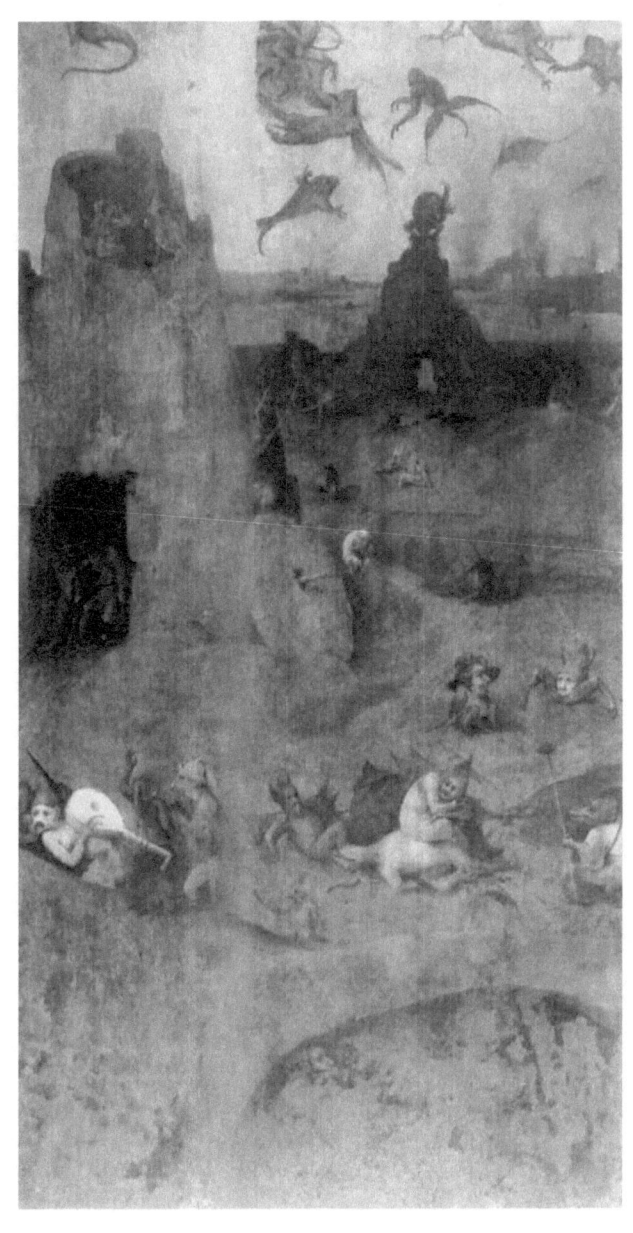

The Fall of the Rebel Angels (obverse)
1500-04, Oil on panel, 69 x 35 cm

There are two panels in Rotterdam thought to have belonged to a triptych the central panel of which is lost. The panel is painted both sides, the obverse sides representing the Fall of the Rebel Angels and Noah's Ark on Mount Ararat, respectively, while on the reverse sides two tondos each representing scenes of Mankind Beset by Devils.

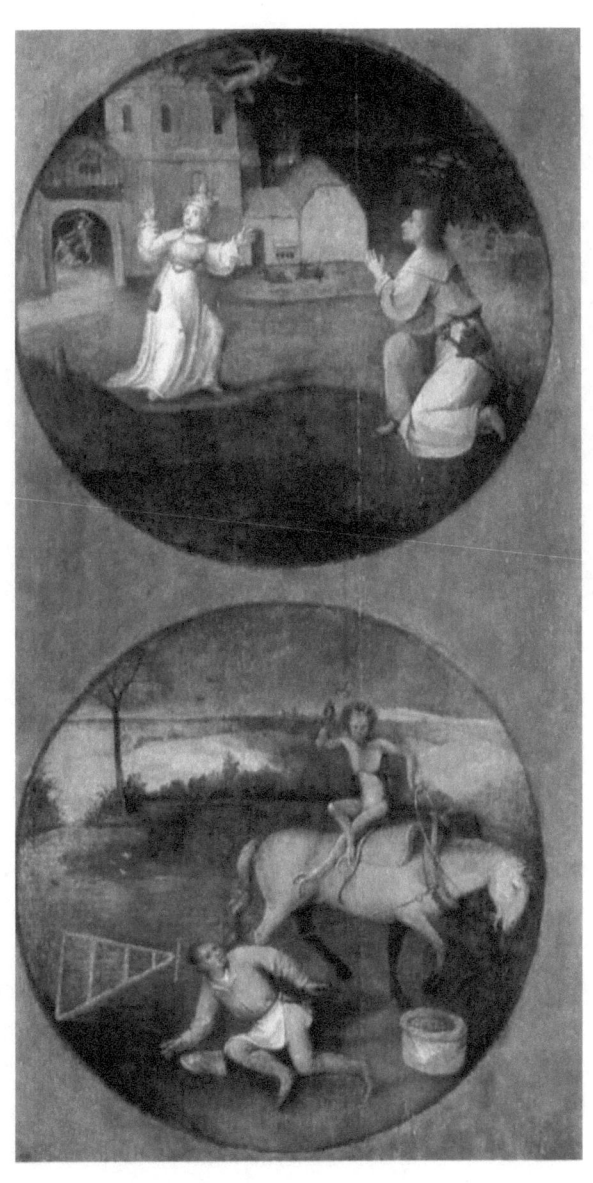

Mankind Beset by Devils (reverse of Rebel Angels
panel)
1500-04, Oil on panel, diameter 32,4 cm (each)

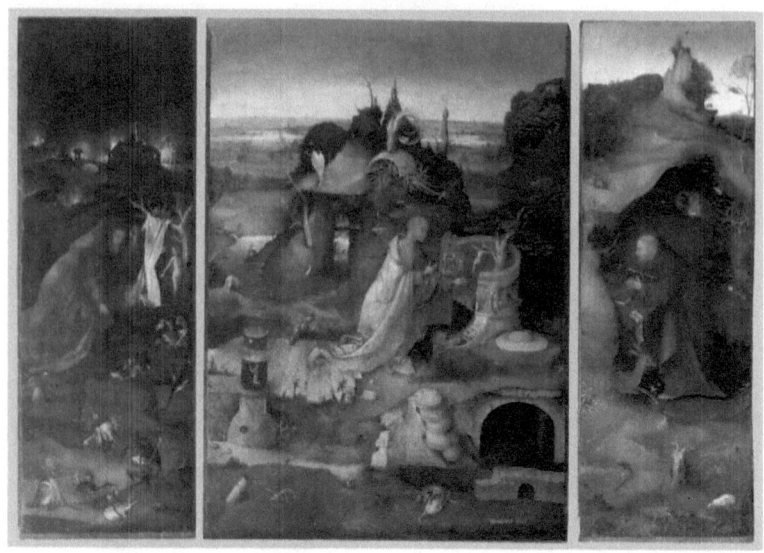

Hermit Saints Triptych
c. 1505, Oil on panel, 86 x 50 cm (centre), 86 x 29 cm
(sides

The Hermit Saints Triptych was painted towards the
middle of Bosch's career. It is perhaps the most
important results of Bosch's stay in Venice. Here he
enlarged the view of the landscape and sought to
capture atmospheric effects. The painting is full of
those bizarre and disquieting apparitions that are a
distinctive feature of his works.

In the centre St Jerome fastens his gaze on a crucifix, secure against the evil world symbolized by the remains of a pagan temple scattered around him on the ground and by two monstrous animals engaged in a death struggle below. On the left, St Anthony the Hermit resists the amorous advances of the Devil-Queen. Snugly ensconced in a cave chapel on the right wing, St Giles prays before an altar, the arrow piercing his breast commemorating the time when he was shot accidentally by a passing hunter. All three saints reflect the monastic ideal: a life spent in mortification of the flesh and in continuous prayer and meditation.

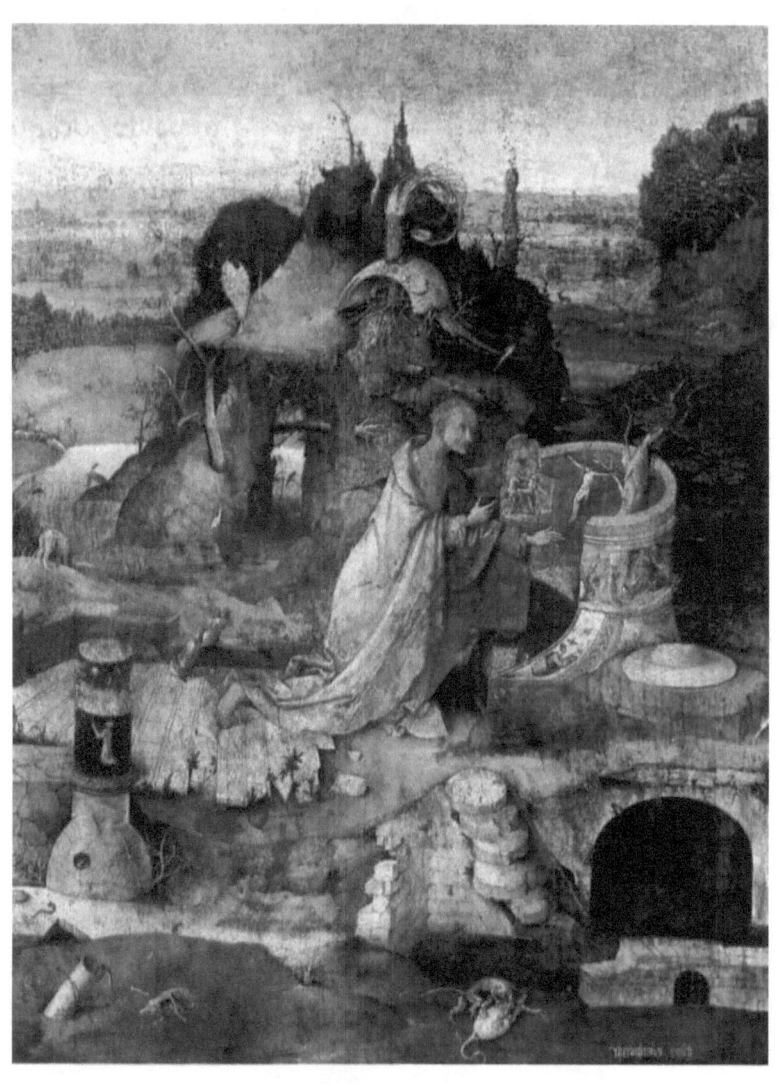

Hermit Saints Triptych (central panel)
c. 1505, Oil on panel, 86 x 50 cm

In the central panel of the triptych St Jerome fastens his gaze on a crucifix, secure against the evil world symbolized by the remains of a pagan temple scattered around him on the ground and by two monstrous animals engaged in a death struggle below.

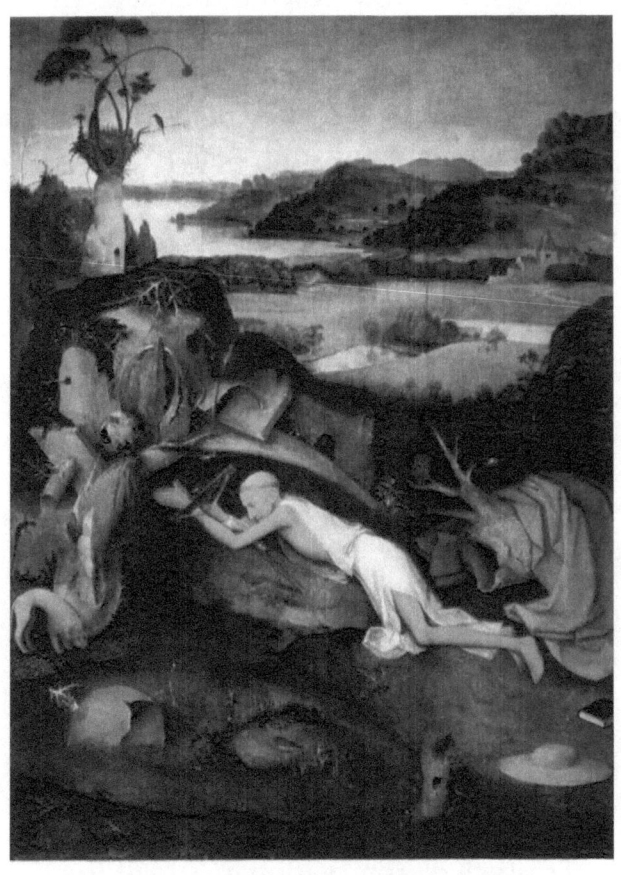

St Jerome in Prayer
c. 1505, Oil on panel, 80, 1 x 60,6 cm

The painting illustrates the contrast between good and evil and between the spirit and the flesh - the principle on which medieval morality was founded. Bosch's painting contrasts Jerome's tribulations in the foreground with a serene landscape that flows away into the background and which is handled with great naturalism. The saint has prostrated himself before a crucifix and finds himself in a strange and poetic setting, full of symbols and attributes. The rocks and tree-trunks are threatening and seem to have come to life, yet, even here, the overall impression is of great realism and lively detail.

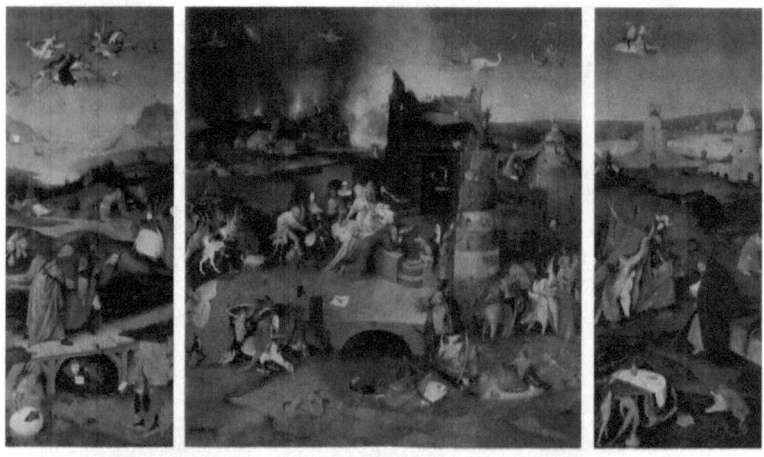

Triptych of Temptation of St Anthony
1505-06, Oil on panel, 131,5 x 119 cm (central), 131,5 x 53 cm (each wing)

Bosch often represented saints in landscapes charged with evil. Nowhere, however, were the vicissitudes of the spiritual life more vividly and circumstantially detailed than in the legend of St Anthony the Hermit, founder of Christian monasticism, which Bosch painted on an altarpiece now preserved in Lisbon.

Bosch was preoccupied with themes of torment and the sinfulness of man, which replaced earlier, more optimistic visions of Christ and the Virgin with feelings of anxiety, fear, and guilt. His sources for such unusual images were the dark corners of the medieval imagination, the gargoyles and monsters of cathedral decoration, and the marginal illustrations of books and popular prints.

The Lisbon triptych sums up the major themes we encounter in the art of Bosch. The spectacle of sin and folly and the shifting horrors of Hell are joined to the images of the suffering Christ and of the saint firm in his faith against the assaults of the World, the Flesh and the Devil. To an age which believed in the reality of Satan and Hell, and in the imminent appearance of Antichrist with the Last Judgment not far behind, the serene countenance of St Anthony looking at us from his haunted chapel must have offered reassurance and hope.

This painting was possibly one of the works formerly belonging to the Escorial, bought by Damiano de Goes, the Portuguese painter.

Bosch's spiritual heroes were the saints who endured both physical and mental torment, yet remained steadfast. Among the saints, Bosch's favourite was Saint Anthony, the subject of his triptych The Temptation of Saint Anthony.

St Anthony (Anthony the Great, or Anthony the Abbot, 251-356) was a Christian saint and hermit, born in Upper Egypt. On the death of his parents he distributed his property among the poor and retired into the Egyptian desert where he remained in solitude for many years. He is generally regarded as the founder of monasticism. During an epidemic, said to be erysipelas, in Europe in the 11th century many cures were claimed in his name and the disease became known as St Anthony's fire. Anthony, like some other hermits, was subject to vivid hallucinations resulting from his ascetic life in the desert. These 'temptations' assume two forms in art, assault by demons and erotic visions.

The triptych features physical punishment on the left wing, a Black Mass in the centre, and the blandishments of food and sex on the right wing. St Anthony's triumph over such trials is mirrored by those of other hermit saints and by the Passion of Christ, whose arrest and carrying of the cross adorn the exterior of the Lisbon altarpiece.

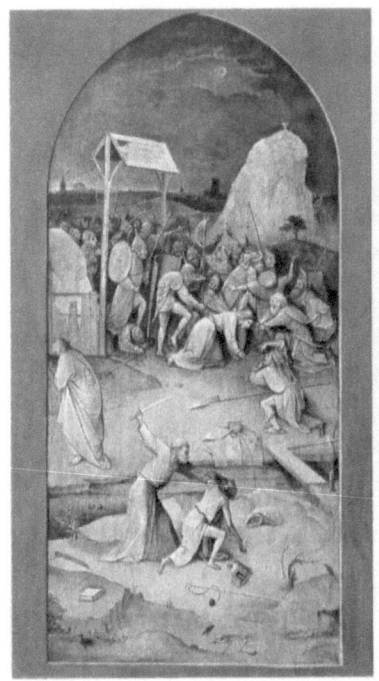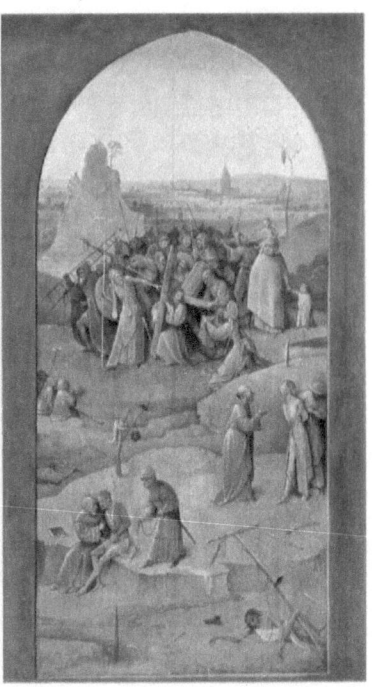

Tiptych of Temptation of St Anthony (outer wings)
1505-06, Grisaille on panel, 131 x 53 cm

The outer wings of the triptych represent the Arrest of
Christ in the Garden of Gethsemane (left wing) and
Christ Carrying the Cross (right wing).

It is most appropriate, that Anthony's sufferings are echoed on the exterior of the altarpiece in two grisaille scenes from Christ's Passion. On the left, soldiers overwhelm Christ in the Garden of Gethsemane as viciously as the devils attack Anthony on the reverse, while Judas hurriedly steals away with his thirty pieces of silver. In the other panel, Christ's collapse beneath the weight of his Cross has halted the procession to Golgotha, allowing St Veronica to wipe the sweat from the Saviour's face. The executioners can hardly restrain their impatience at this delay, and the bystanders look on more with idle curiosity than with sympathy Below, the two thieves confess to hooded friars whose disreputable characters have been deftly portrayed.

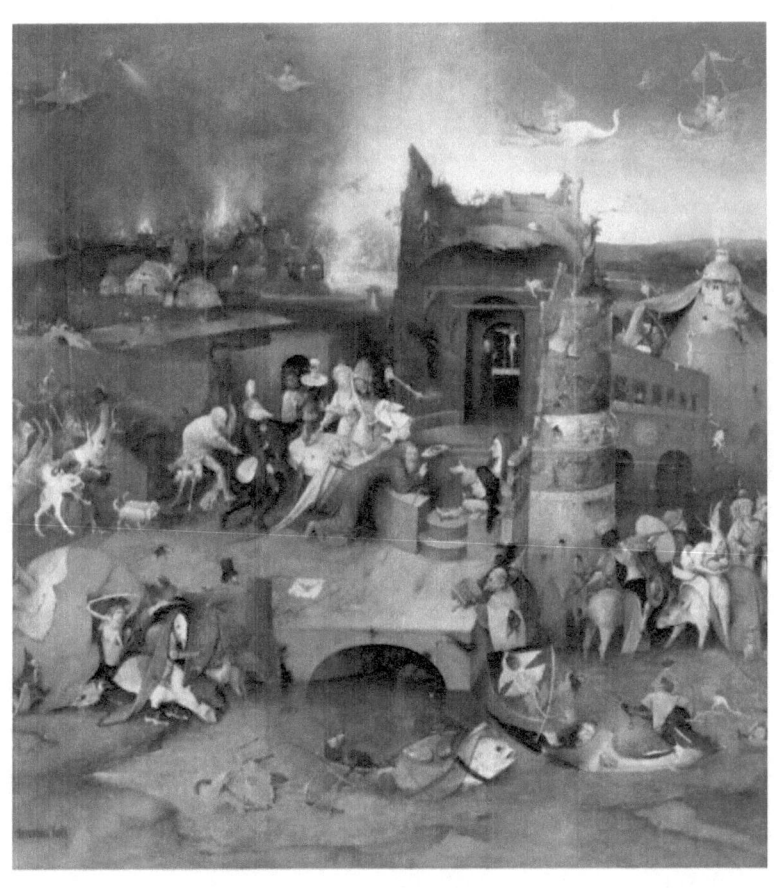

Triptych of Temptation of St Anthony (central panel)
1505-06, Oil on panel, 131 x 119 cm

The diabolic enterprises represented in the triptych reach a climax in the middle panel. Devils of all species, human and grotesque, arrive from all directions by land, water and air, to converge upon a ruined tomb in the centre. On a platform before the tomb, an elegantly dressed pair have set up a table from which they dispense drink to their companions. Near by, a woman wearing a large headdress and a gown with an extravagantly long train kneels at a parapet to offer a bowl to a figure opposite. Kneeling beside her, almost unnoticed in the midst of this hellish activity, is St Anthony himself; he turns towards the viewer, his right hand raised in blessing. His gesture is echoed by Christ half-hidden in the depths of the tomb, which Anthony has converted into a chapel. The right wall of the sanctuary ends in a decaying tower covered with monochrome scenes. Two of them, the Adoration of the Golden Calf and a group of men making offerings to an enthroned ape, are images of idolatry, while the third, the Israelites returning from Canaan with a bunch of grapes, prefigures Christ carrying the Cross on the outer wings of the triptych.

A burning village illuminates the dusky background, probably a reference to the disease of ergotism or "St Anthony's Fire", whose victims invoked the name of St Anthony for relief. The ancient association of ergotism with the devil-plagued saint may have been influenced by the fact that one phase of the disease is characterized by hallucinations in which the sufferer believes that he is attacked by wild beasts or demons.

The devils who have gathered around St Anthony display a complexity of form unusual even for Bosch. In the group far right, for example, a blasted tree trunk becomes the bonnet, torso and arms of a woman whose body terminates in a scaly lizard tail; she holds a baby and is mounted on a giant rat. Near by, a jug has been transformed into another beast of burden whose wholly unsubstantial rider bears a thistle for a head. In the water below, a man has been absorbed into the interior of a gondola-fish, his hands thrust helplessly through its sides. An armoured demon with a horse's skull for a head plays a lute at lower left; he sits astride a plucked goose who wears shoes and whose neck ends in a sheep's muzzle. All these shifting forms, moreover, display a richness of colour that confers a visual beauty on even the most disgusting shape. A recent, careful cleaning of the triptych, among Bosch's best preserved works, reveals brilliant reds and greens alternating with subtly modulated passages of blue-greys and browns.

This convocation of fiends ostensibly illustrates the second attack on Anthony described in the literary accounts; the miraculous light which dispersed the devils on this occasion can be seen shining through one of the chapel windows. But the devils do not seem about to scatter "like dust in the wind", as one version has it, nor are they physically attacking Anthony. Instead, their torments must be understood in a spiritual sense. Like the monstrous creatures who confront Deguilleville's pilgrim, they are incarnations of the sinful urges with which Anthony wrestled in his desert solitude. In a drawing made around 1500, Albrecht Dьrer similarly illustrated the evil thoughts of a group of people at Mass by means of little devils fluttering about their heads. A number of sins symbolized by Bosch's monsters can be identified, chief among which is Lust. Lust is also represented more overtly in the group of buildings at extreme right, where a monk and a prostitute drink together within a tent; there may be a further reference in the dark-skinned devil in the central group: the demon of unchastity, we are told, once appeared to Anthony in the form of a black boy. It should not be surprising that even the most ascetic saints were susceptible to this particular vice: as the "Malleus Maleficarum" informs us, it was through the carnal act that the Devil could most easily assail mankind.

Anthony, however, has overcome all his temptations through the strength of his faith. This faith is expressed in his gesture of benediction, thought to be particularly efficacious against the Devil; and the steady gaze which the hermit directs towards us is one of comforting assurance. While the wings of the Lisbon triptych show Anthony tempted and tormented, the central panel thus shows him triumphant.

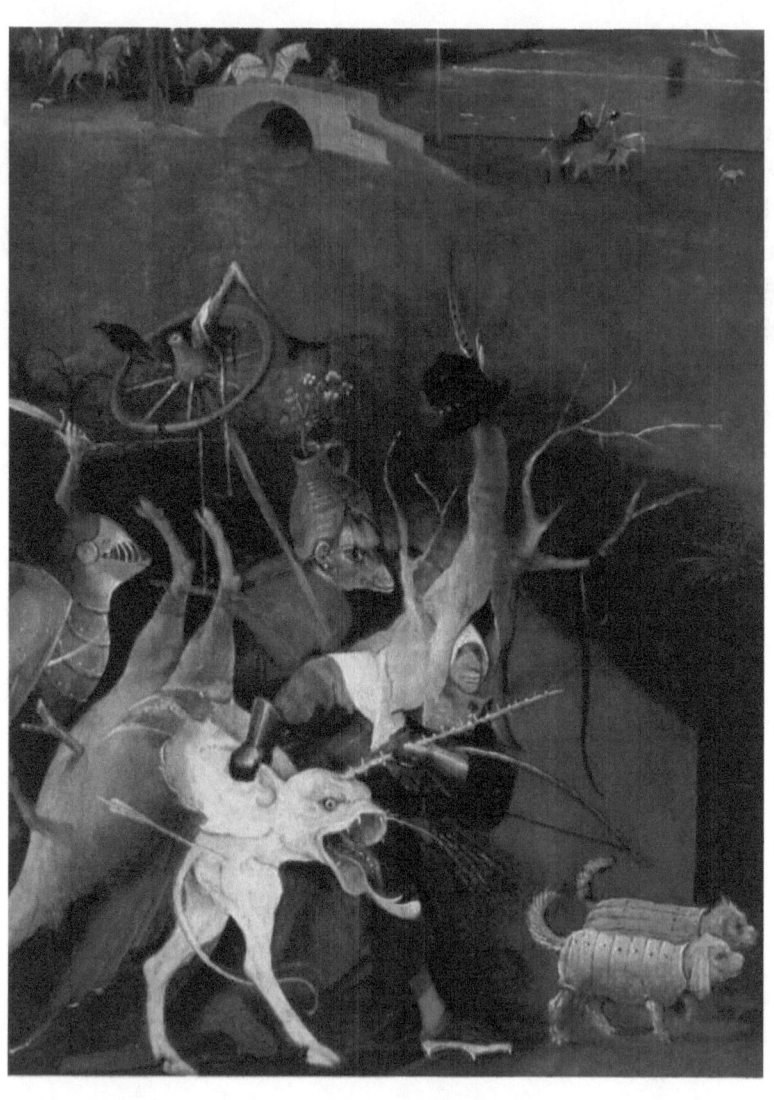

Triptych of Temptation of St Anthony (detail)
1505-06, Oil on panel

The picture shows a detail of the central panel, which represents the Group of the Vengeance Spirits. Devils of all species, human and grotesque, arrive from all directions by land, water and air, to converge upon a ruined tomb in the centre.

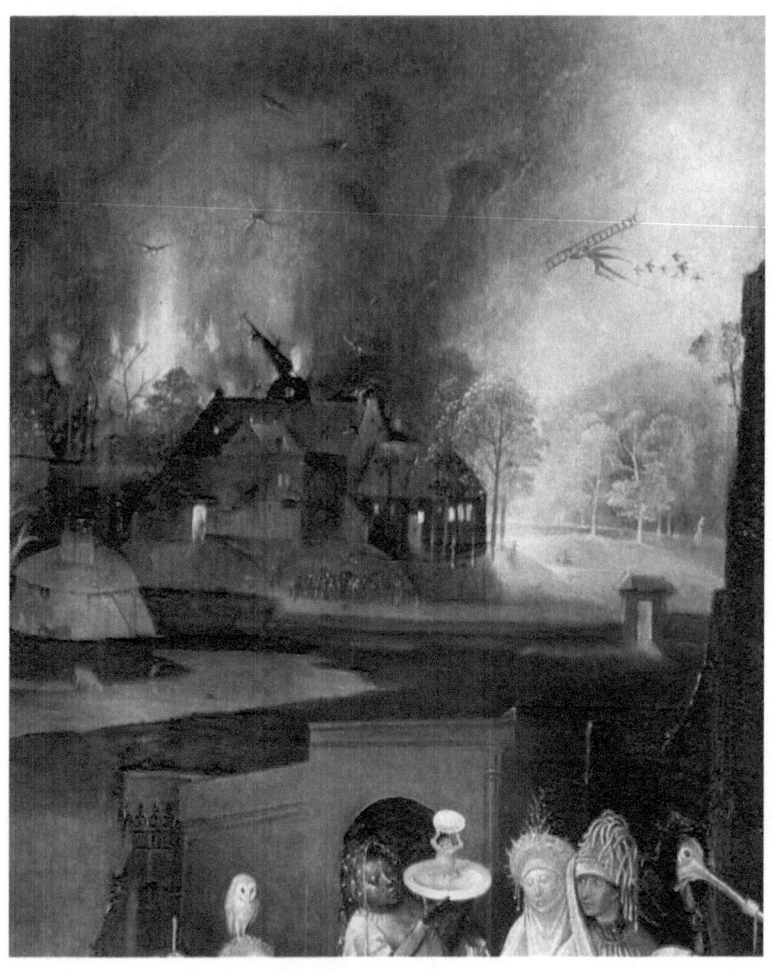

Triptych of Temptation of St Anthony (detail)
1505-06, Oil on panel

The picture shows a detail of the central panel, which represents the Fire of the Cloister. A burning village illuminates the dusky background, probably a reference to the disease of ergotism or "St Anthony's Fire", whose victims invoked the name of St Anthony for relief.

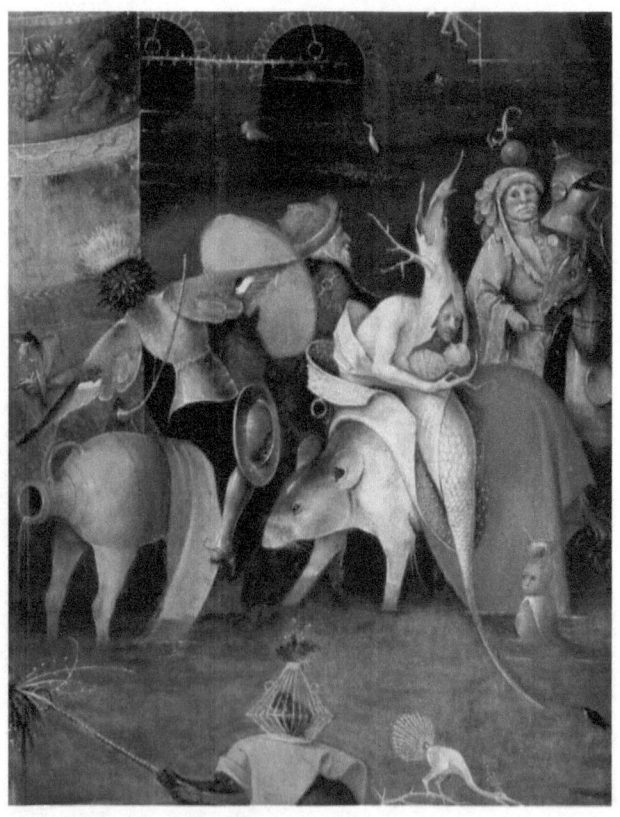

Triptych of Temptation of St Anthony (detail)
1505-06, Oil on panel

he picture shows a detail of the central panel, which represents the Choir of Offering. In the group far right, a blasted tree trunk becomes the bonnet, torso and arms of a woman whose body terminates in a scaly lizard tail; she holds a baby and is mounted on a giant rat.

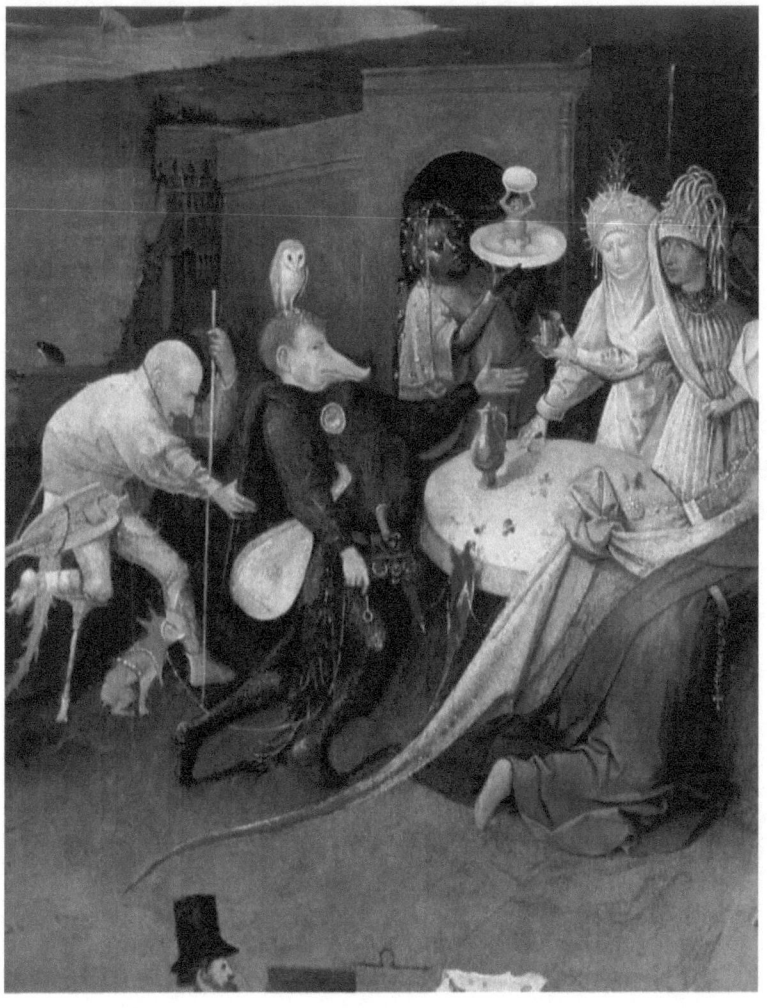

Triptych of Temptation of St Anthony (detail)
1505-06, Oil on panel

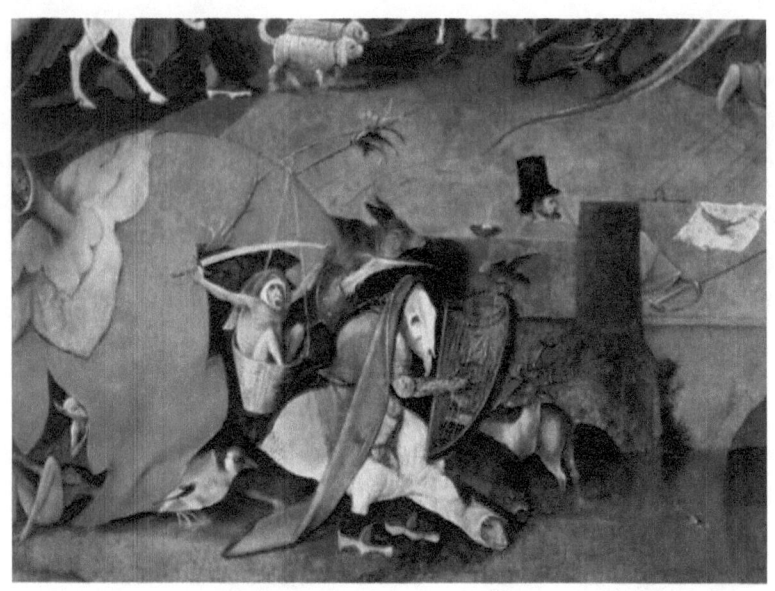

Triptych of Temptation of St Anthony (detail)
1505-06, Oil on panel
The picture shows a detail of the central panel, which depicts the Mandragora in Murky Pool.

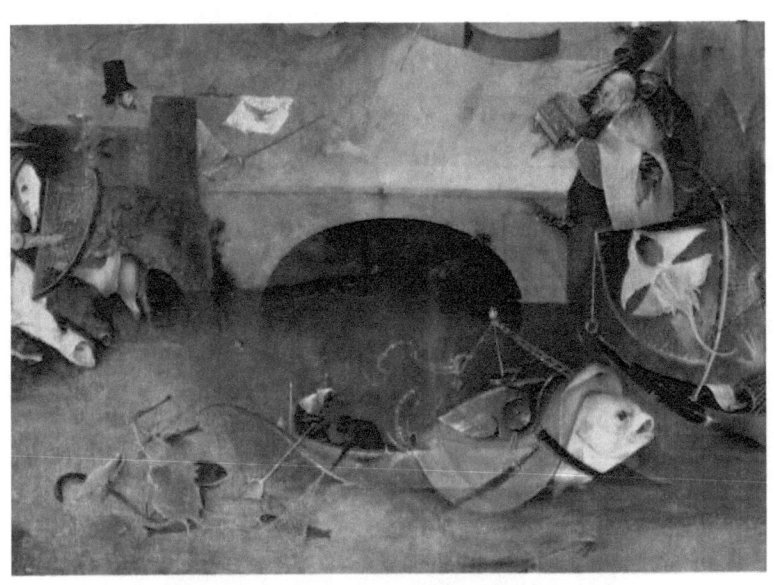

Triptych of Temptation of St Anthony (detail)
1505-06, Oil on panel
The picture shows a detail of the central panel, which depicts the Carp Ship.

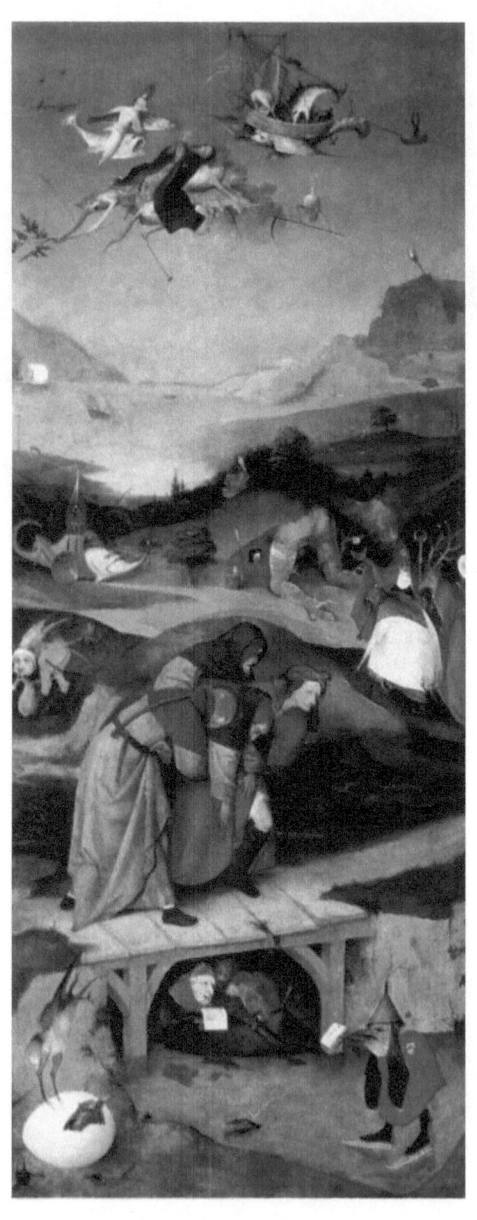

Triptych of Temptation of St Anthony (left wing)
1505-06, Oil on panel, 131, 5 x 53 cm

The left wing of the triptych represents the Flight and Failure of St Anthony.

As we learn from medieval compendia of saints' lives, St Anthony passed most of his long life (c. 251 -356) in the Egyptian desert, where his extraordinary piety made him an object of special attention for Satan. Once while praying in the shelter of an old tomb, Anthony was overwhelmed by a horde of devils who beat him so relentlessly that he was left for dead. After several fellow hermits had rescued and revived him, however, he returned to the tomb, where the devils caught him a second time and tossed him high into the air. This time his torments ended only when a Divine light illuminated the tomb and dispersed the devils. Satan then appeared in the guise of a beautiful and saintly queen whom Anthony encountered bathing in a river. Taking the hermit into her city, the Devil-Queen showed him all her supposed works of charity, and it was only when she sought to seduce the bedazzled Anthony that he recognized her true nature and intentions.

Two of these episodes are represented on the left inner wing of the Lisbon altarpiece. In the foreground, the unconscious Anthony is carried across a bridge by two companions dressed in the habit of the Antonite Order, accompanied by a secular figure that has been identified with some plausibility as a self-portrait of Bosch. Anthony appears again in the sky, borne aloft by demons, while other monsters buzz around him like angry insects. These scenes conform fairly closely to the written sources but as in so many other instances, Bosch enriched the original accounts with a wealth of inventive and dramatic detail. Three monsters confer beneath the bridge as an equally grotesque messenger skates towards them on the ice. A bird gulps down its newly hatched young at lower left. On the road ahead of Anthony and his companions, another group of demons approach a kneeling male figure whose body forms the roof and entrance of a brothel; a false beacon lures ships to their destruction in the sea beyond; and the shore is littered with corpses.

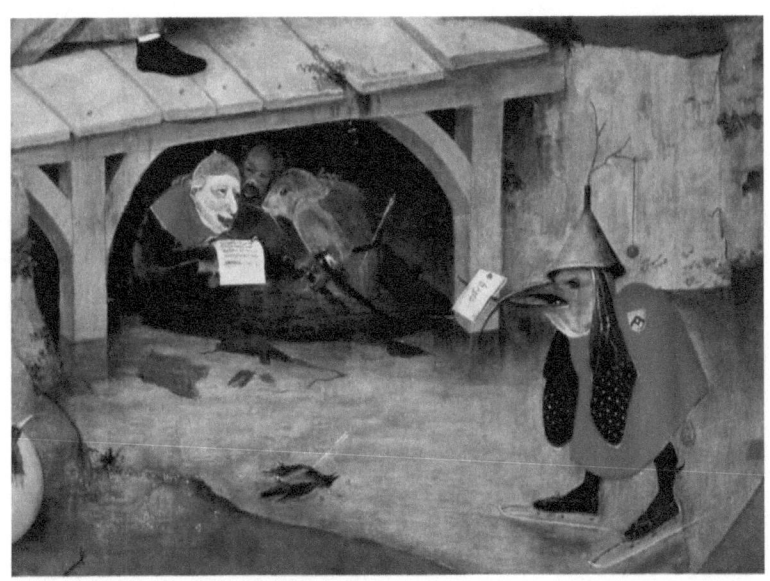

Triptych of Temptation of St Anthony (detail)
1505-06, Oil on panel

The picture shows a detail of the left wing, the
Conspiracy under the Footbridge. Three monsters
confer beneath the bridge as an equally grotesque
messenger skates towards them on the ice.

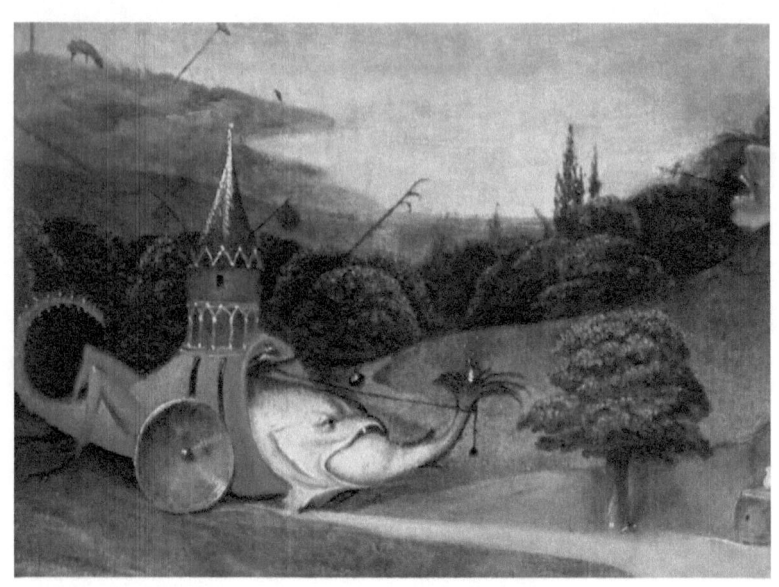

Triptych of Temptation of St Anthony (detail)
1505-06, Oil on panel
The picture shows a detail of the left wing, representing
the Leviathan.

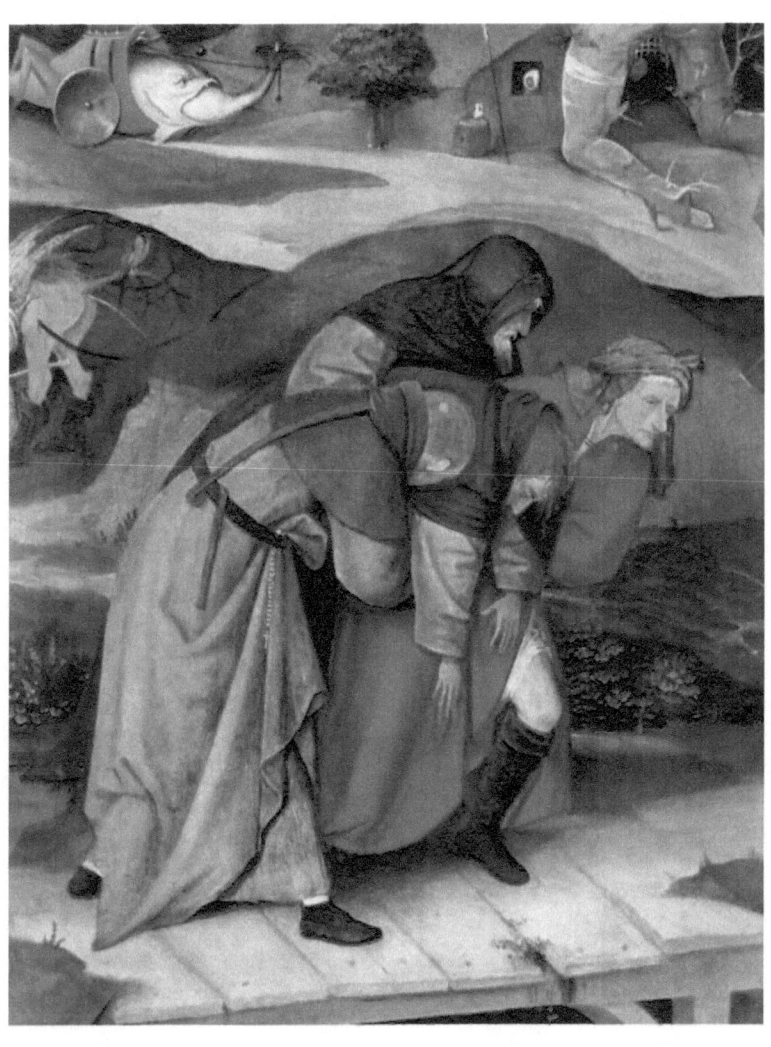

Triptych of Temptation of St Anthony (detail)
1505-06, Oil on panel

The picture shows a detail of the left wing, depicting the Rescue. In the foreground, the unconscious Anthony is carried across a bridge by two companions dressed in the habit of the Antonite Order, accompanied by a secular figure who has been identified with some plausibility as a self-portrait of Bosch.

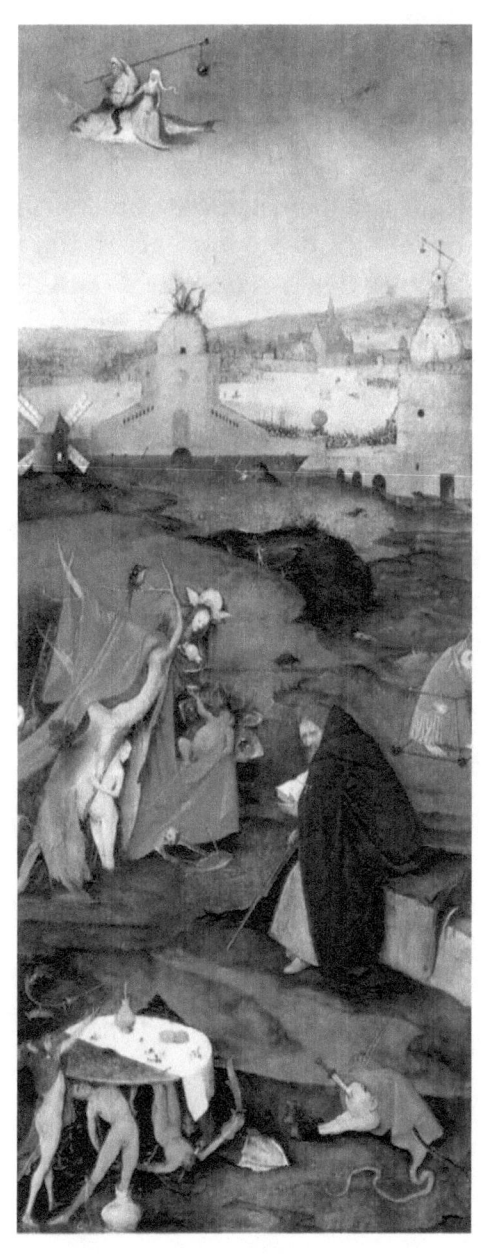

Triptych of Temptation of St Anthony (right wing)
1505-06, Oil on panel, 131,5 x 53 cm

The right wing represents St Anthony in Meditation. The powerful evocation of a corrupt and stinking world is no less apparent in the right wing, where Bosch used as his starting point the story of the Devil-Queen, a subject he had already depicted in the Hermit Saints altarpiece. The Devil-Queen appears in the river before Anthony, shielding her private parts with a false modesty and surrounded by her infernal court. Anthony averts his eyes from this obscene group only to be summoned by a demon-herald to the devilish feast in the foreground. The open-air table, the cloth slung tent-like over the tree stump beside the temptress, and the servants pouring wine seem like a grotesque parody of the traditional Garden of Love. In the background looms the city of the Devil-Queen, its demonic nature betrayed by the dragon swimming in the moat and by the flames erupting from the top of the main gate.

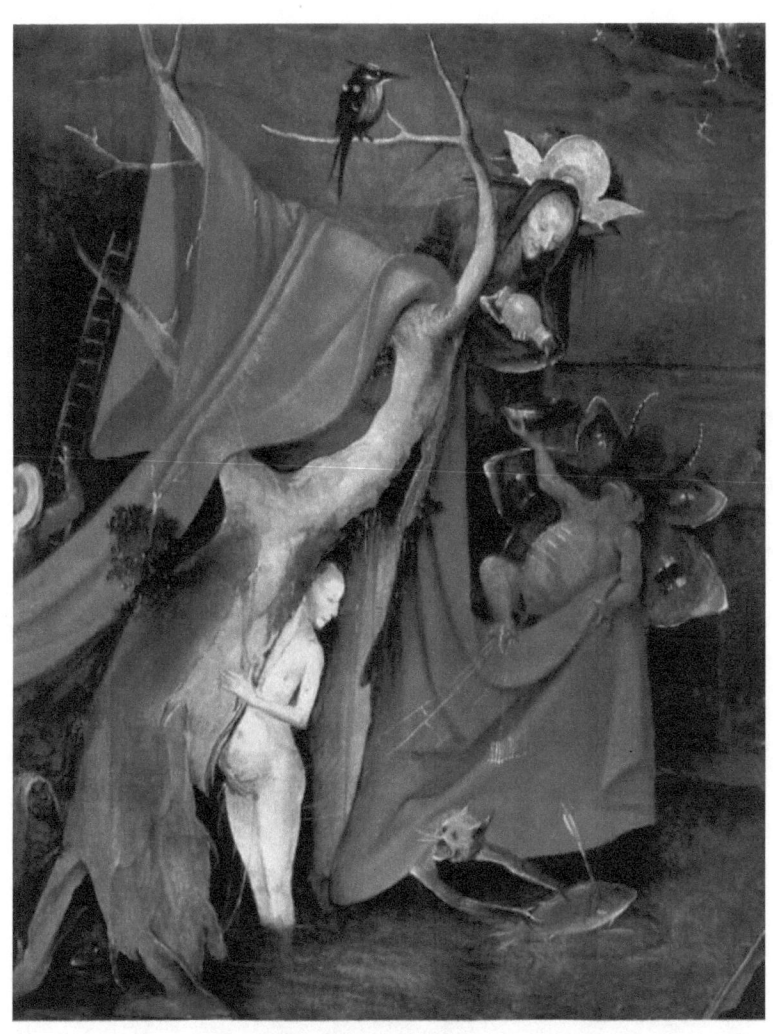

Triptych of Temptation of St Anthony (detail)
1505-06, Oil on panel
The picture shows a detail of the right wing, depicting
the Wedding of the Frogs. The Devil-Queen appears in
the river before Anthony, shielding her private parts
with a false modesty and surrounded by her infernal
court.

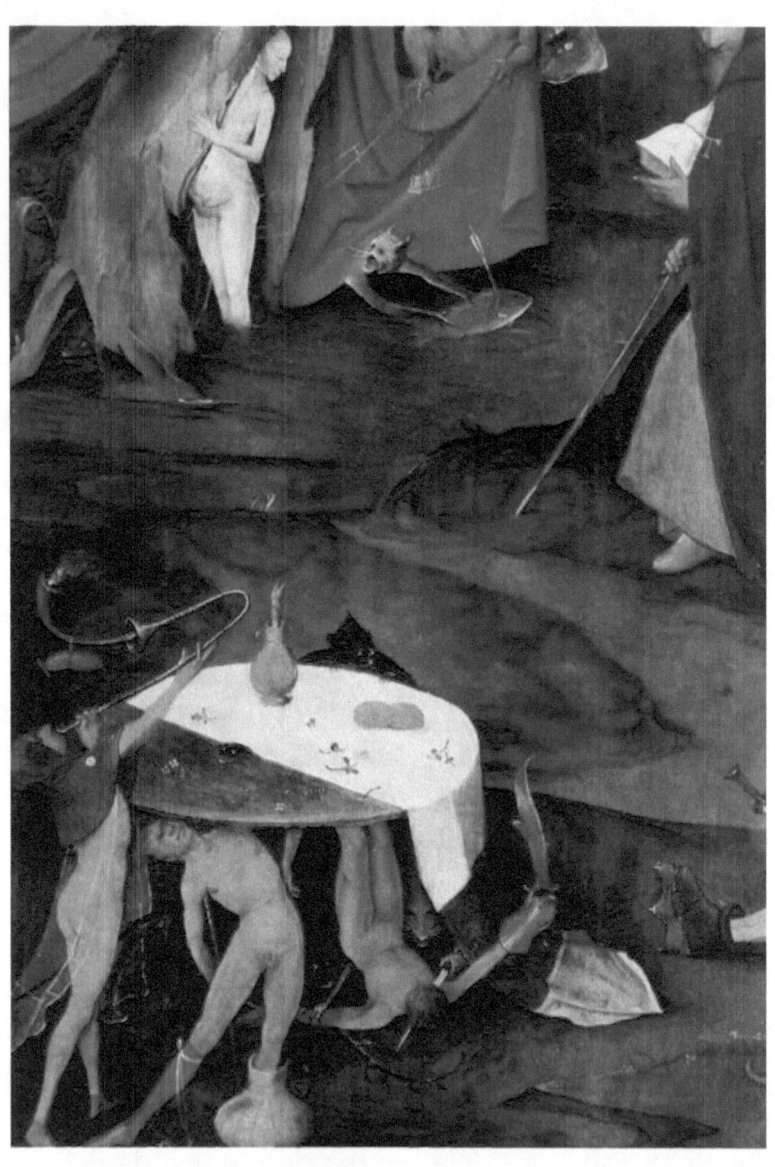

Triptych of Temptation of St Anthony (detail)
1505-06, Oil on panel

The picture shows a detail of the right wing. The open-air table, the cloth slung tent-like over the tree stump beside the temptress, and the servants pouring wine seem like a grotesque parody of the traditional Garden of Love.

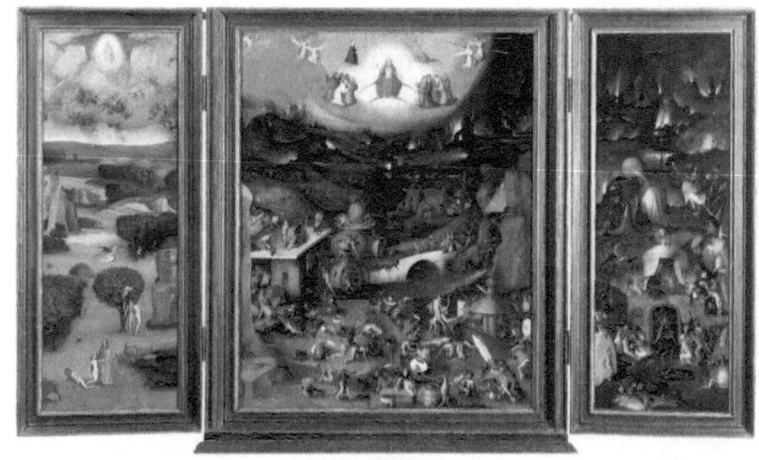

Last Jjudgment Triptych
1504-08, Mixed technique on panel, 163 x 128 cm
(central panel), 167 x 60 cm (each wing)

While sin and folly occupy a prominent place in Bosch's art, their significance can be fully appreciated only within the context of a larger medieval theme, the Last Judgment. The preparation for this Final Day was one of the chief concerns of the medieval Church. In Bosch's days the terrors of the Final Reckoning were intensified by a general sense of its imminence. Nowhere, however, was this chronic anxiety of the age given more vivid expression than in Bosch's imposing Last Judgment triptych in Vienna, executed probably during his middle period.

The central panel of the triptych represents the Last Judgment and the Seven Deadly Sins. The interior view of the left wing depicts the Fall of the Rebel Angels, Creation of Eve, Fall of Man and Expulsion, while the interior view of the right wing shows Hell and the Prince of Darkness.

The inclusion of the Fall of Adam and Eve in a representation of the Last Judgment is unusual; the other two panels of the Vienna triptych depart even more from traditional iconography. Generally Heaven was allotted the chief role in the eschatological drama. As in the altarpiece by Roger van der Weyden, it is the act of judgment which is stressed; the judged are relegated to positions of secondary importance, and the felicity of the saved is described as fully as the pains of the lost. In Bosch's version, however, the divine court appears small and insignificant at the top of the central panel, and very few souls are numbered among the elect. The majority of mankind has been engulfed in the universal cataclysm which rages throughout the deep, murky landscape below.

This vast panoramic nightmare represents the earth in her final death throes, destroyed not by water as Dьrer and Leonardo were to envision it, but by the fire foretold in a thirteenth-century hymn, the sombre Dies Irae: "Day of Wrath, that day when the world dissolves in glowing ashes". Bosch was probably also influenced by the account of the last days given in the Revelation of St John, a book which enjoyed renewed popularity in the late fifteenth century, when it was illustrated by Dьrer in his famous Apocalypse woodcuts of 1497-98. The wide valley dominating the central panel may represent the Valley of Jehoshaphat, which, on the basis of several Old Testament references (Joel 4:2,12), was traditionally thought to be the site of the Last Judgment, with the walls of the earthly Jerusalem blazing in the background. In any event, earth has become indistinguishable from Hell, depicted on the right wing, out of which the army of Satan swarms to attack the damned; the eternity of torment has begun.

The Hell scene in the Prado Tabletop had paired off each punishment with one of the Deadly Sins. In the Last Judgment it would be difficult to identify the punishments with specific sins. The avaricious are boiled in the great cauldron just visible beneath one of the buildings in the central panel. Around the corner, a fat glutton is forced to drink from a barrel held by two devils; the source of his dubious refreshment can be seen squatting in the window overhead. The lascivious woman on the roof above suffers the attentions of a lizard-like monster slithering across her loins, while being serenaded by two musical demons. On the cliffs to the right, across the river, blacksmith-devils hammer other victims on anvils, and one is being shod like a horse; these unfortunate souls are guilty of the sin of anger.

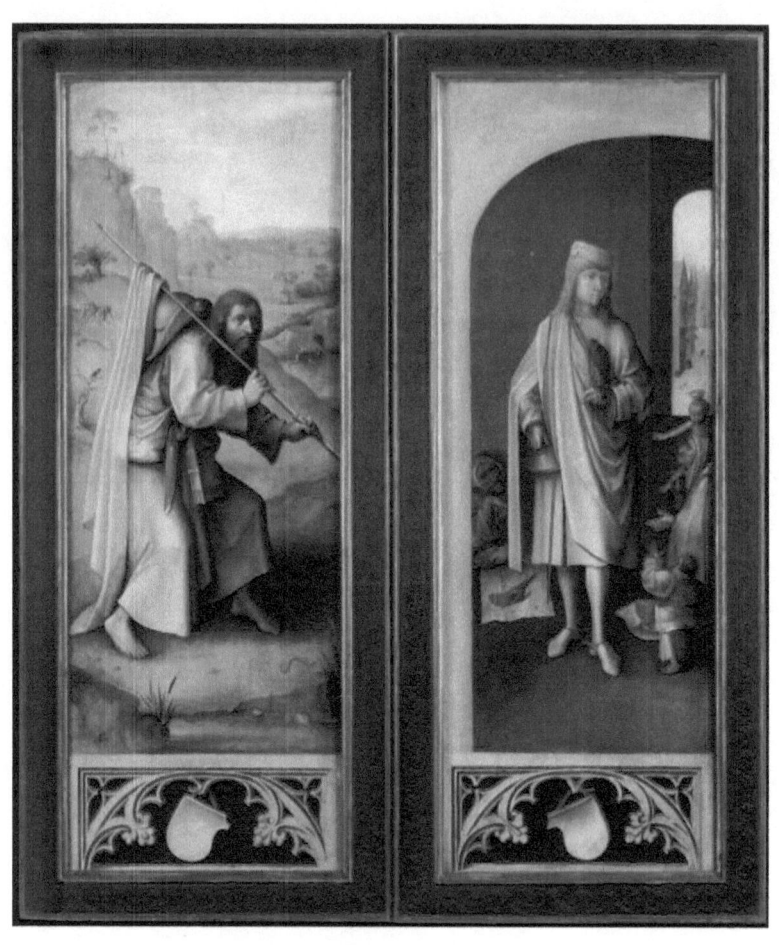

Last Jjudgment Triptych (exterior view)
1504-08, Grisaille on panel

The reverse sides of the wings, painted in grisaille (seen when the triptych is closed) depict St James the Greater on Pilgrimage and St Bavo Giving Alms to the Poor and Sick.

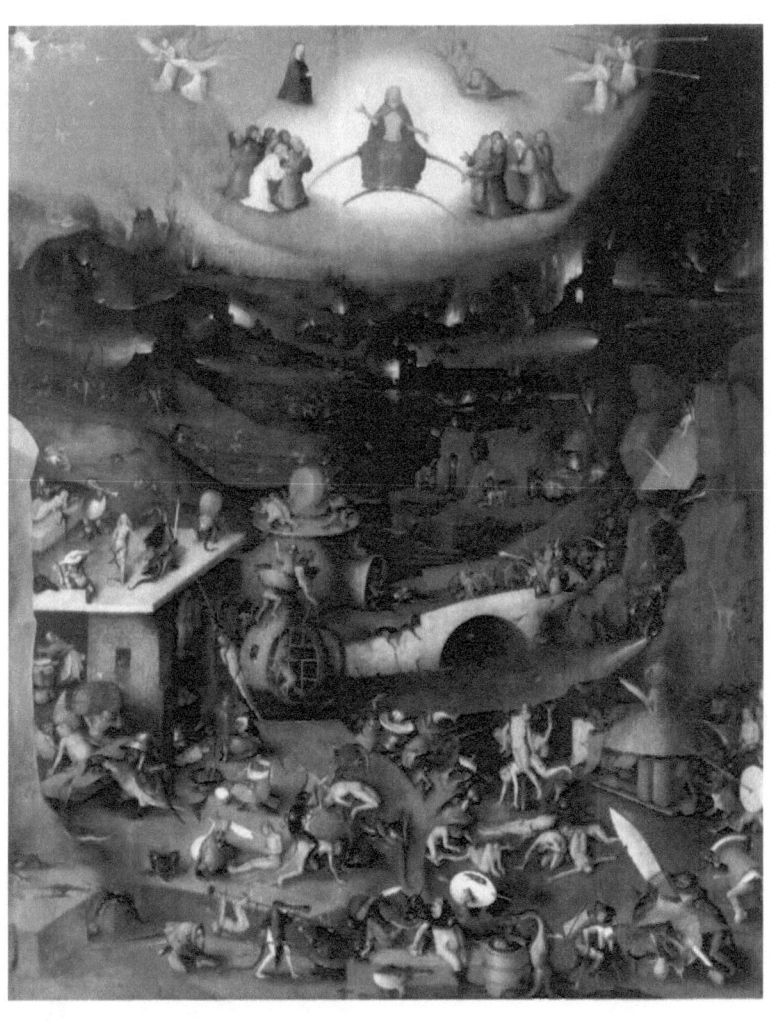

Last Jjudgment Triptych (central panel)
1504-08, Mixed technique on panel, 163 x 128 cm

This vast panoramic nightmare represents the earth in her final death throes, destroyed not by water as Dьrer and Leonardo were to envision it, but by the fire foretold in a thirteenth-century hymn, the sombre Dies Irae: "Day of Wrath, that day when the world dissolves in glowing ashes". Bosch was probably also influenced by the account of the last days given in the Revelation of St John, a book which enjoyed renewed popularity in the late fifteenth century, when it was illustrated by Dьrer in his famous Apocalypse woodcuts of 1497-98. The wide valley dominating the central panel may represent the Valley of Jehoshaphat, which, on the basis of several Old Testament references (Joel 4:2,12), was traditionally thought to be the site of the Last Judgment, with the walls of the earthly Jerusalem blazing in the background. In any event, earth has become indistinguishable from Hell, depicted on the right wing, out of which the army of Satan swarms to attack the damned; the eternity of torment has begun.

The Hell scene in the Prado Tabletop had paired off each punishment with one of the Deadly Sins. In the Last Judgment it would be difficult to identify the punishments with specific sins. The avaricious are boiled in the great cauldron just visible beneath one of the buildings in the central panel. Around the corner, a fat glutton is forced to drink from a barrel held by two devils; the source of his dubious refreshment can be seen squatting in the window overhead. The lascivious woman on the roof above suffers the attentions of a lizard-like monster slithering across her loins, while being serenaded by two musical demons. On the cliffs to the right, across the river, blacksmith-devils hammer other victims on anvils, and one is being shod like a horse; these unfortunate souls are guilty of the sin of anger.

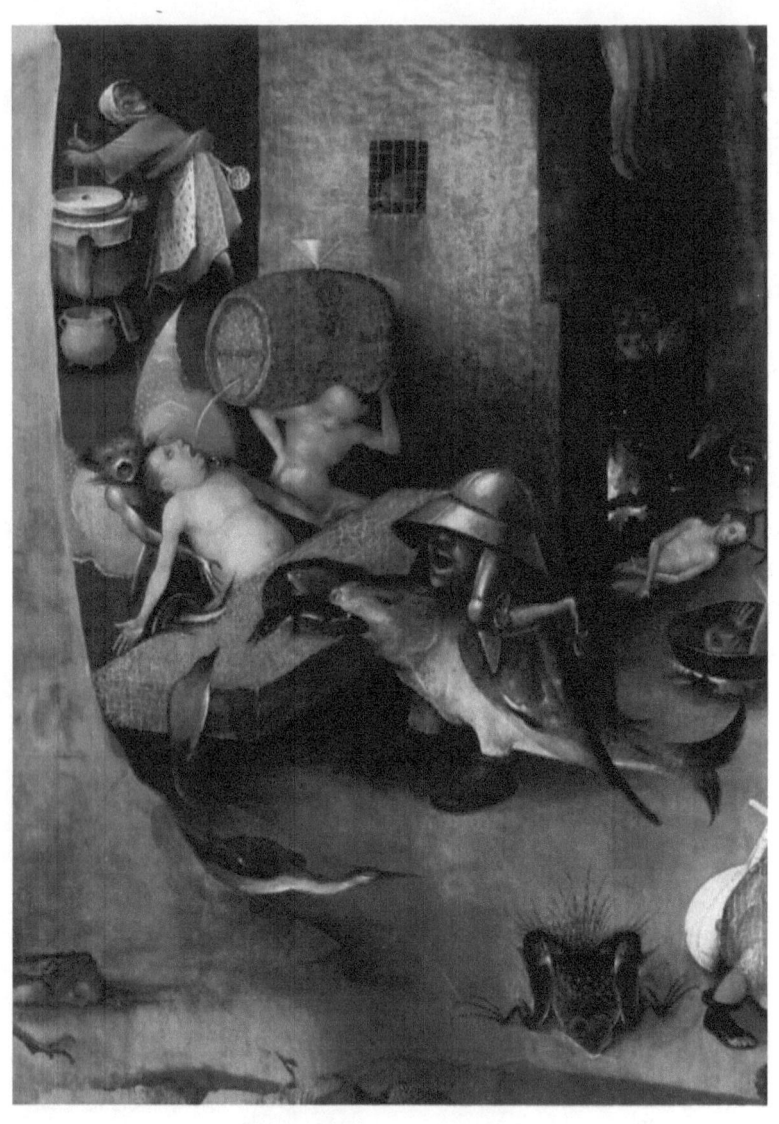

Last Jjudgment Triptych (detail)
1504-08, Mixed technique on panel

The detail from the central panel depicts the sin of Gluttony and its punishment. Around the corner, a fat glutton is forced to drink from a barrel held by two devils; the source of his dubious refreshment can be seen squatting in the window overhead.

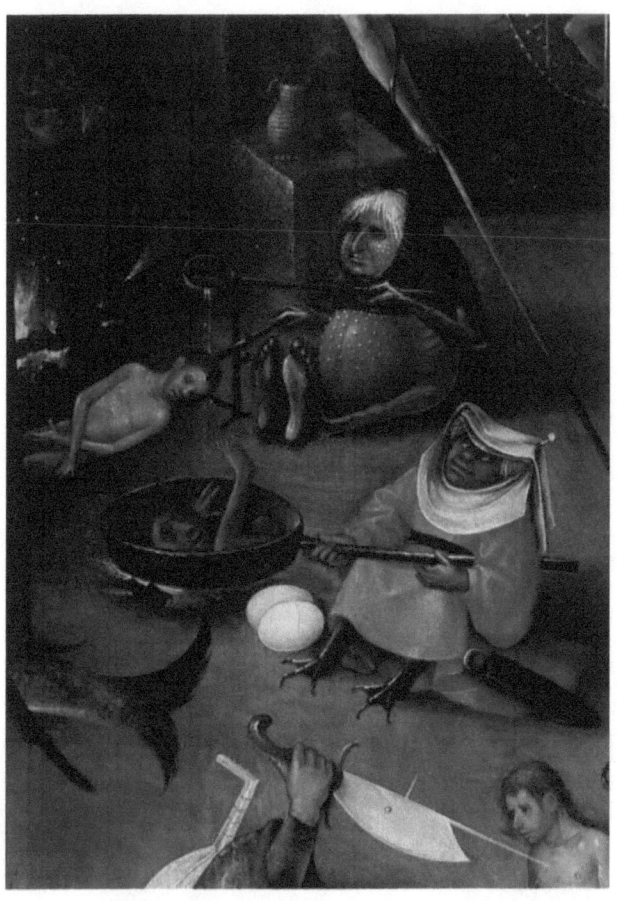

Last Jjudgment Triptych (detail)
1504-08, Mixed technique on panel

The detail from the central panel depicts the sin of Avarice and its punishment. The avaricious are boiled in the great cauldron just visible beneath one of the buildings in the central panel. The cauldron is filled with the molten metal of their money assets.

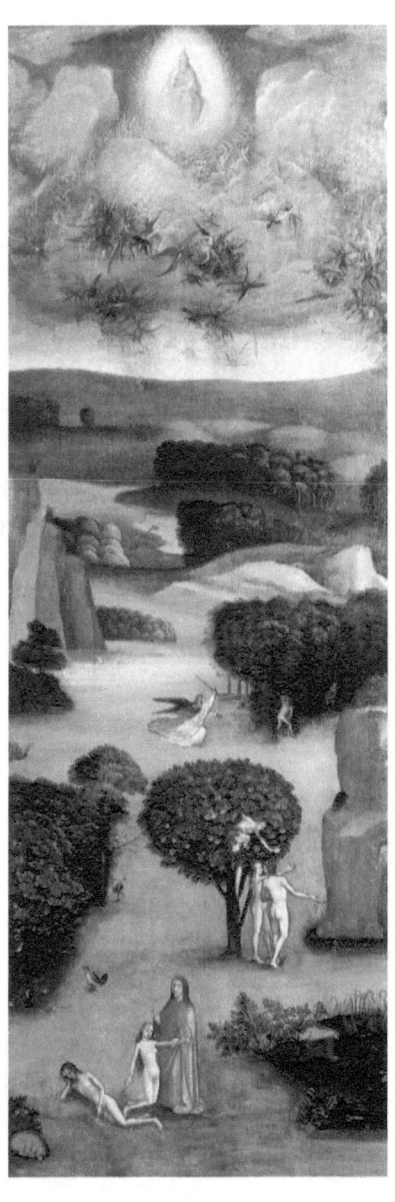

Last Jjudgment Triptych (left wing)
1504-08, Mixed technique on panel, 167 x 60 cm

The left wing of the triptych represents the Paradise. Here, across the three inner panels, appear the First and Last Things, beginning with the Fall of Man on the left wing.

The story recounted in the second and third chapters of Genesis has been placed in a lush garden; in the foreground we see the creation of Eve, followed by the temptation of the First Couple. In the middle distance they are driven from the garden by an angel. The expulsion of Adam and Eve from Eden is paralleled above by the expulsion from Heaven of the Rebel Angels, who are transformed into monsters as they descend to earth. Although the revolt of proud Lucifer and his followers is not mentioned in Genesis, it appears in Jewish legends and entered Christian doctrine at an early age. These were the angels who sinned and whose prince, envying Adam, caused him to sin in turn. It was further believed that Adam and Eve had been created by God in order that their offspring might fill the places left vacant by the fallen angels. In this panel, Bosch thus depicted the entrance of sin into the world and accounted for the necessity of the Last Judgment.

The inclusion of the Fall of Adam and Eve in a representation of the Last Judgment is unusual; the other two panels of the Vienna triptych depart even more from traditional iconography.

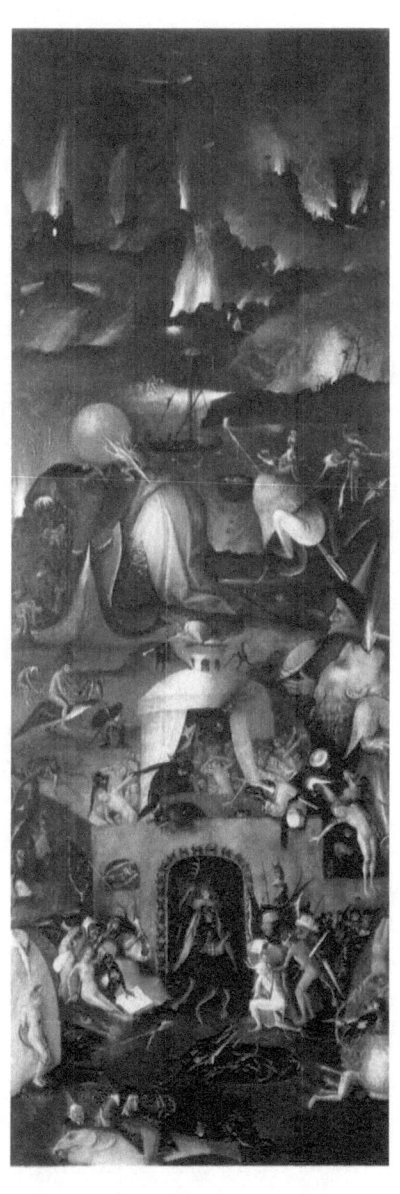

Last Jjudgment Triptych (right wing)
1504-08, Mixed technique on panel, 167 x 60 cm

The right wing of the triptych represents the Hell.

Bosch must have been familiar with contemporary texts describing Hell. Their influence can be seen not only in his rendering of specific punishments, but also in the general topography of his Hell, including such features as the burning pits and furnaces, and the lakes and rivers in which the damned are immersed. Some of his monsters are also derived from traditional literary and visual sources. The vaguely anthropomorphic devils occur in many earlier Last Jjudgment scenes. Traditional, too, are the toads, adders and dragons which crawl over the rocks or gnaw at the vital parts of their victims.

Into this more or less conventional fauna of Hell, however, Bosch introduced new and more frightening species whose complex forms defy precise description. Many display bizarre fusions of animal and human elements, sometimes combined with inanimate objects. To this group belongs the bird-like monster who helps carry a giant knife in the centre panel; his torso develops into a fish tail and two humanoid legs, shod in a pair of jars. To the right an upturned basket darts forward on legs, a sword clutched in its mailed fist. Disembodied heads scuttle about on stubby limbs; others possess bodies and limbs which glow in the darkness. Several fiends blow musical instruments thrust into their hind quarters, bringing to mind the farting devil encountered by Dante (Inferno, XXI, 139).

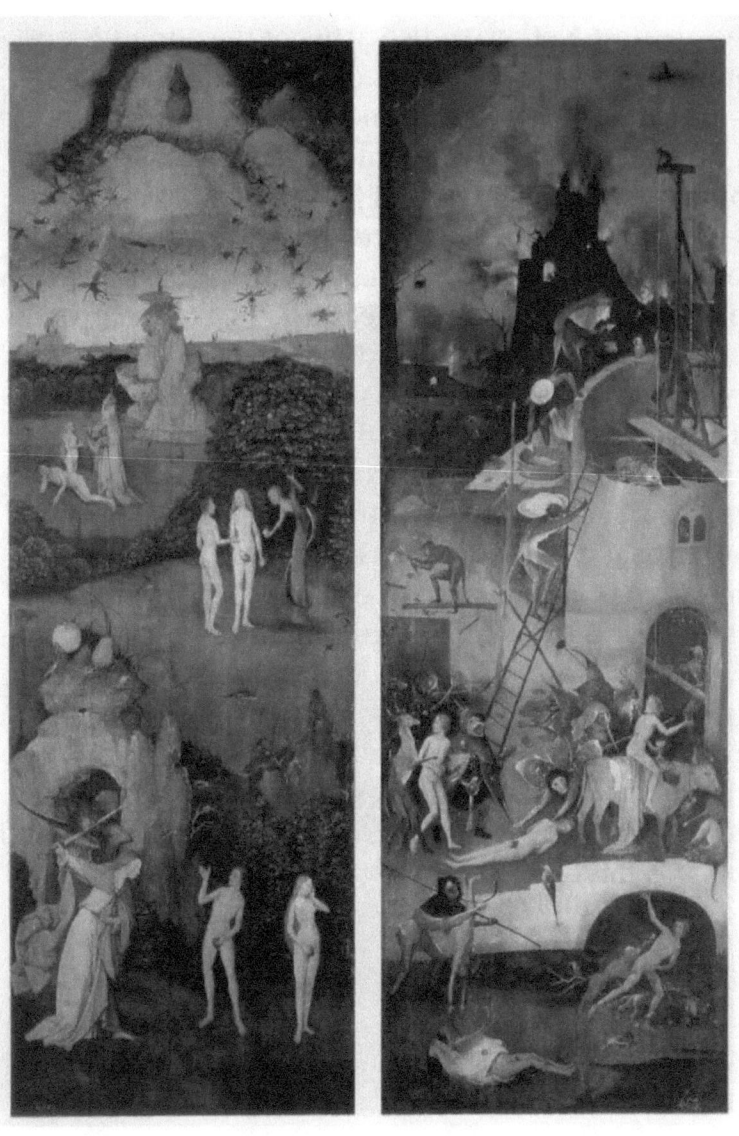

Paradise and Hell
c. 1510, Oil on wood, 135 x 45 cm (each panel)
The two panels once were the left and right wings of a
triptych.

The greatest Netherlandish artist of the period is not found among the adherents of the New Style but among those who, like Grunewald in Germany, refused to be drawn into the modern movement from the South. In the Dutch town of 's Hertogenbosch there lived such a painter, who was called Hieronymous Bosch. Very little is known about him. We do not know how old he was when he died in 1516, but he must have been active for a considerable time since he became an independent master in 1486. Like Grunewald, Bosch showed that the traditions and achievements of painting which had been developed to represent reality most convincingly could be turned round, as it were, to give us an equally plausible picture of things no human eye had seen. He became famous for his terrifying representations of the powers of evil. Perhaps it is no accident that the gloomy King Philip II of Spain, later in the century, had a special predilection for this artist, who was so much concerned with man's wickedness. These two pictures show two wings from one of Bosch's triptychs Philip bought and which is therefore still in Spain.

On the left we watch evil invading the world. The creation of Eve is followed by the temptation of Adam and both are driven out of Paradise, while high above in the sky we see the fall of the rebellious angels, who are hurled from heaven as a swarm of repulsive insects. On the other wing we are shown a vision of hell. There we see horror piled upon horror, fires and torments and all manner of fearful demons, half animal, half human or half machine, who plague and punish the poor sinful souls for all eternity. For the first and perhaps for the only time, an artist had succeeded in giving concrete and tangible shape to the fears that had haunted the minds of man in the Middle Ages. It was an achievement which was perhaps only possible at this very moment, when the old ideas were still vigorous and yet the modern spirit had provided the artist with methods of representing what he saw. Perhaps Hieronymus Bosch could have written on one of his paintings of hell what Jan van Eyck wrote on his peaceful scene of the Arnolfinis' betrothal: 'I was there'.

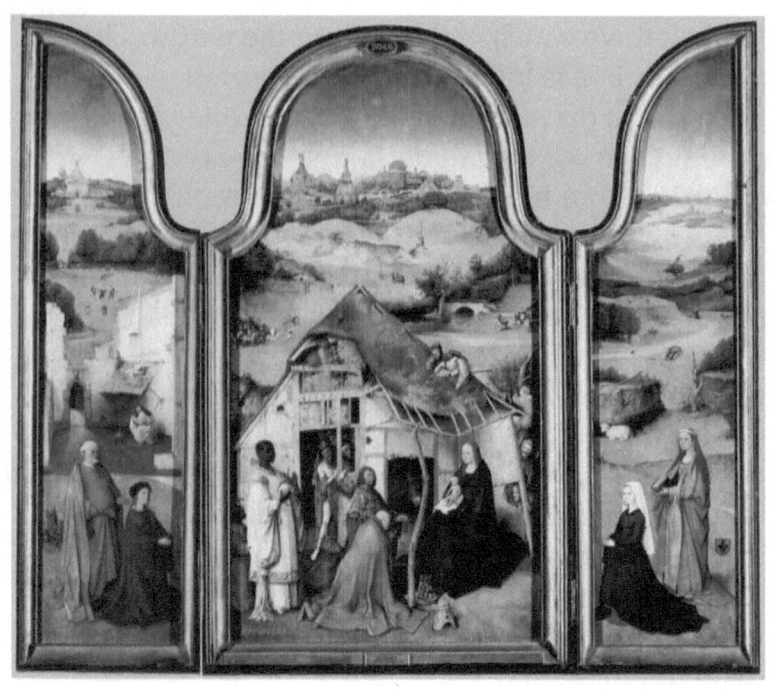

Triptych of the Adoration of the Magi
c. 1510, Oil on wood, 138 x 72 cm (central), 138 x 34 cm
(each wings)

The inner wings of this altarpiece are occupied by the
kneeling figures of the donors, husband and wife,
attended by their patron saints Peter and Agnes. The
coats of arms behind them identify the couple as
members of the Bronckhorst and Bosshuyse families,
but nothing is known of these names which would help
determine the date of the work or its original
destination.

The central panel displays the adoration of the Christ Child by the three Kings or Magi. The Infant Christ sits solemnly enthroned on his mother's lap. The Virgin and Child resemble a cult statue beneath its baldachin, and the Magi approach with all the gravity of priests in a religious ceremony. The splendid crimson mantle of the kneeling King echoes the monumental figure of the Virgin. That Bosch intended to show a parallel between the homage of the Magi and the celebration of the Mass is clearly indicated by the gift which the oldest King has placed at the feet of the Virgin: it is a small sculptured image of the Sacrifice of Isaac, a prefiguration of Christ's sacrifice on the Cross. Other Old Testament episodes appear on the elaborate collar of the second King, representing the visit of the Queen of Sheba to Solomon, and on the Moorish King's silver orb, depicting Abner offering homage to David.

A group of peasants have gathered around the stable at the right. They peer from behind the wall with lively curiosity and scramble up to the roof in order to get a better view of the exotic strangers. The Shepherds had seen Christ on Christmas Eve, but they frequently reappear as spectators in fifteenth-century Epiphany scenes. Generally, however, they display much more reverence than do Bosch's peasants, whose boisterous behaviour contrasts strongly with the dignified bearing of the Magi.

The most curious detail of Bosch's Epiphany is the man standing just inside the stable behind the Magi. Naked except for a thin shirt and a crimson robe gathered around his loins, he wears a bulbous crown; a gold bracelet encircles one arm, and a transparent cylinder covers a sore on his ankle. He regards the Christ Child with an ambiguous smile, but the faces of several of his companions appear distinctly hostile.

Because they stand within the dilapidated stable, time-honoured symbol of the Synagogue, these grotesque figures have been identified as Herod and his spies, or Antichrist and his counsellors. Although neither identification is quite convincing, the association of the chief figure with the powers of darkness is clearly suggested by the demons embroidered on the strip of cloth hanging between his legs. A row of similar forms can be seen on the large object which he holds in one hand; surprisingly, this can only be the helmet of the second King, and still other monsters decorate the robes of the Moorish King and his servant. These demonic elements undoubtedly refer to the pagan past of the Magi.

The stable and its inhabitants seem to be the source of the malevolent influences contaminating almost every part of the majestic landscape which unfolds in the background of all three panels. Demons haunt the ruined portal in the left wing, where Joseph sits hunched over a fire. The crumbling walls around him are the remains of King David's palace, near which the Nativity was popularly supposed to have occurred; like the stable, it represents the Synagogue, the Old Law collapsing at the advent of the New. In the field beyond, peasants dance to the sound of bagpipes, a familiar symbol of the carnal life. On the right wing, wolves attack a man and a woman on a desolate road. Behind the stable in the centre, the followers of two of the Magi rush towards each other like opposing armies; the host of the third King appears beyond the sand dunes. The gently rolling countryside contains, in addition, an abandoned tavern and a pagan idol. Even the distant grey-blue walls of Jerusalem, one of Bosch's most evocative renderings of the Holy City, appear vaguely sinister. A little roadside cross leans precariously to one side at the left, and the two watch-towers are architecturally similar to the demonic city which Bosch depicted in the St Anthony triptych in Lisbon.

The frame of the triptych is original.

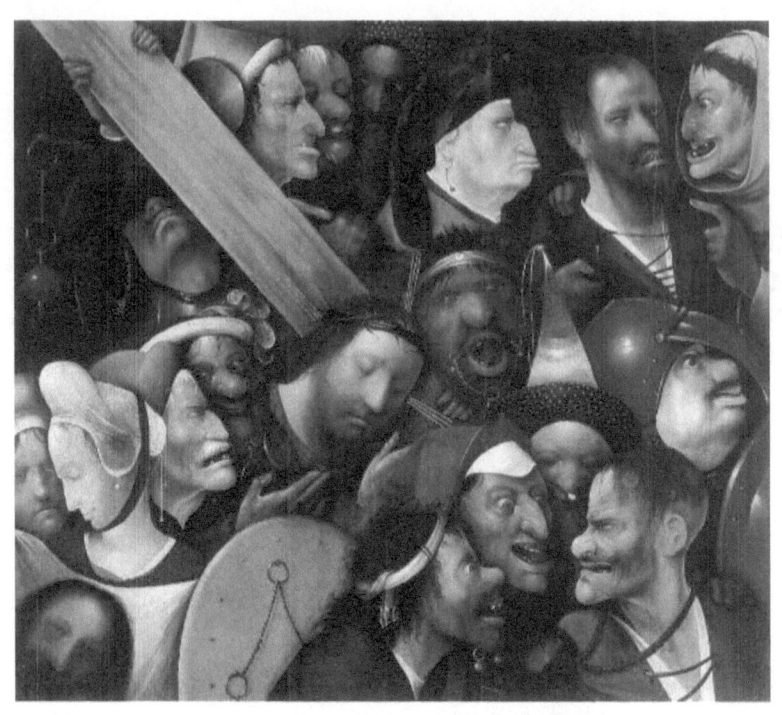

Christ Carrying the Cross
1515-16, Oil on panel, 74 x 81 cm

Christ Carrying the Cross is an exceptionally dramatic painting, with a bold composition made up of closely packed heads for which no parallel exists in the art of the period around 1500. It is generally considered to be a late work and one of Bosch's greatest creations. The antithesis between good and evil, which was so crucial to Christian belief in Bosch's time, is raised to a climax. The painting is a peerless study of human facial expressions and demonic visages. Yet the chaotic and caricatured elements are never overwhelming and the painting seems to observe a complex balance of parallels and contrasts that emphasizes the serenity of Christ's gently modelled face in the centre. Amid all the tumult, we make out the clear profile of St Veronica withdrawing from the mob, the image of Christ's face - the 'vera icon' on her cloth.

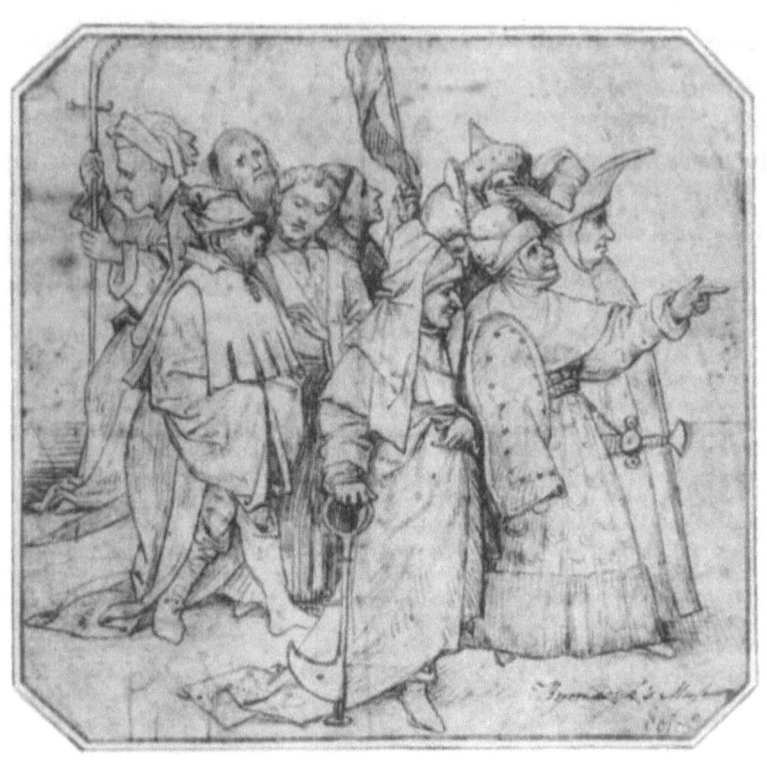

Group of Male Figures, Pen, 124 x 126 mm

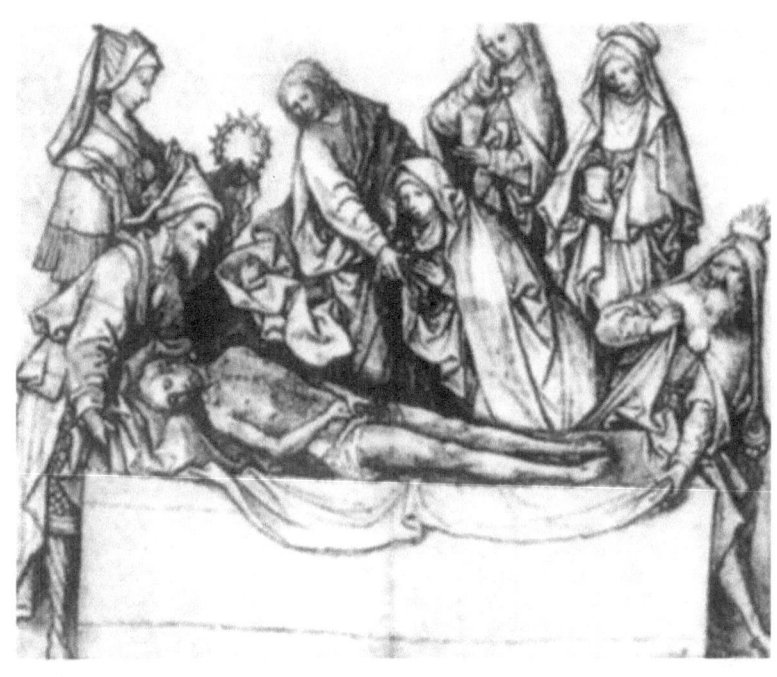

The Entombment, Ink and grey wash, 250 x 350 mm

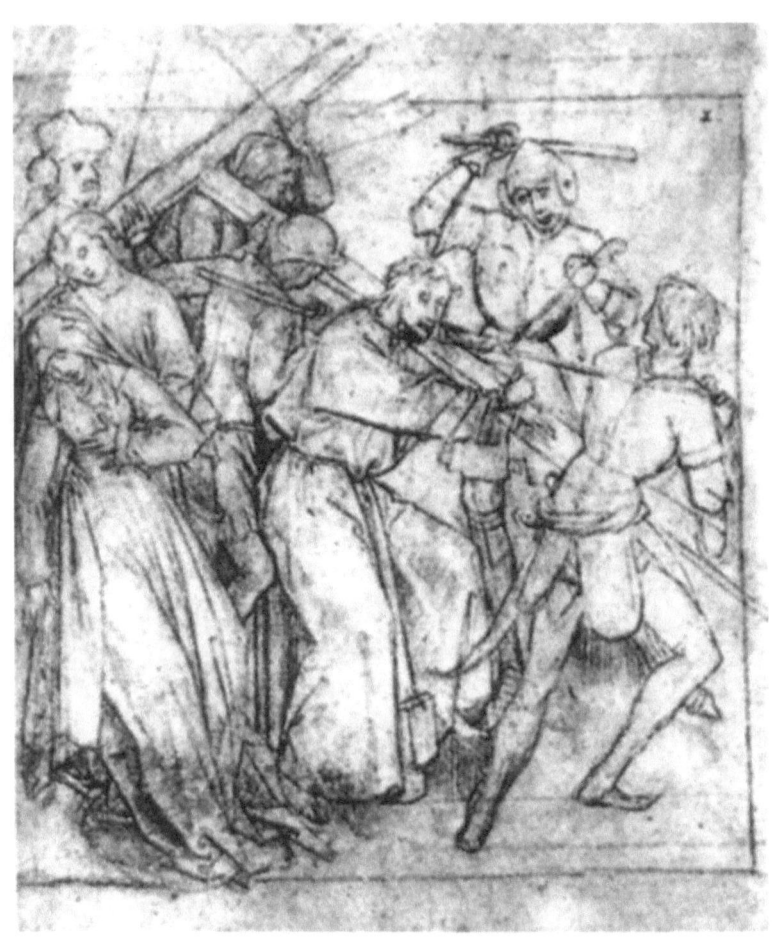

Christ Carrying the Cross, Pen, 236 x 198 mm

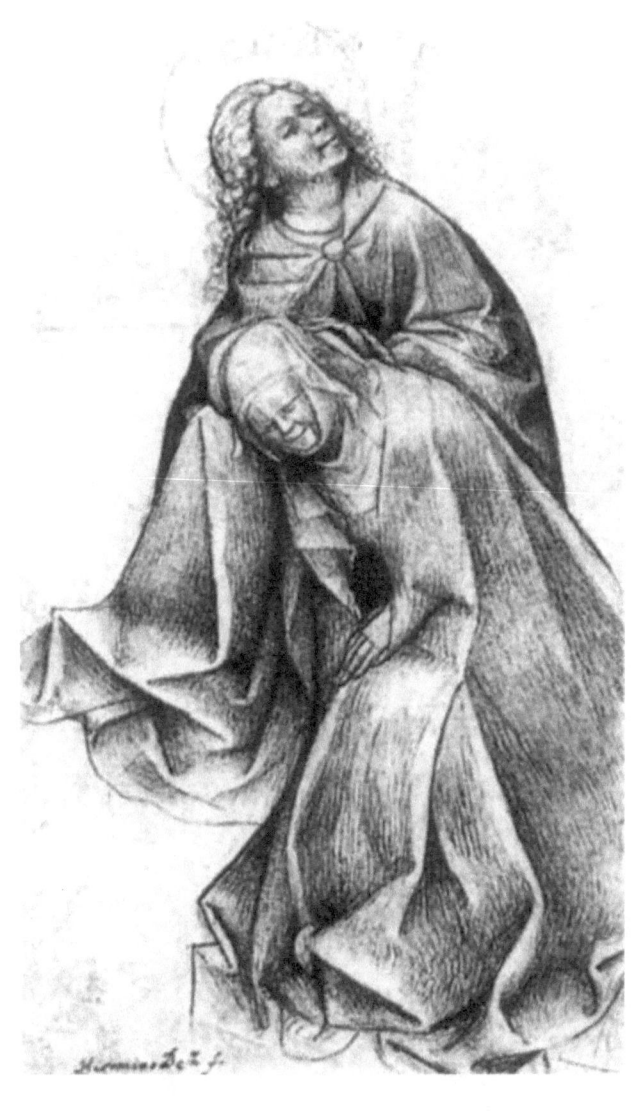

Mary and John at the Foot of the Cross, Brush, 302 x 172 mm

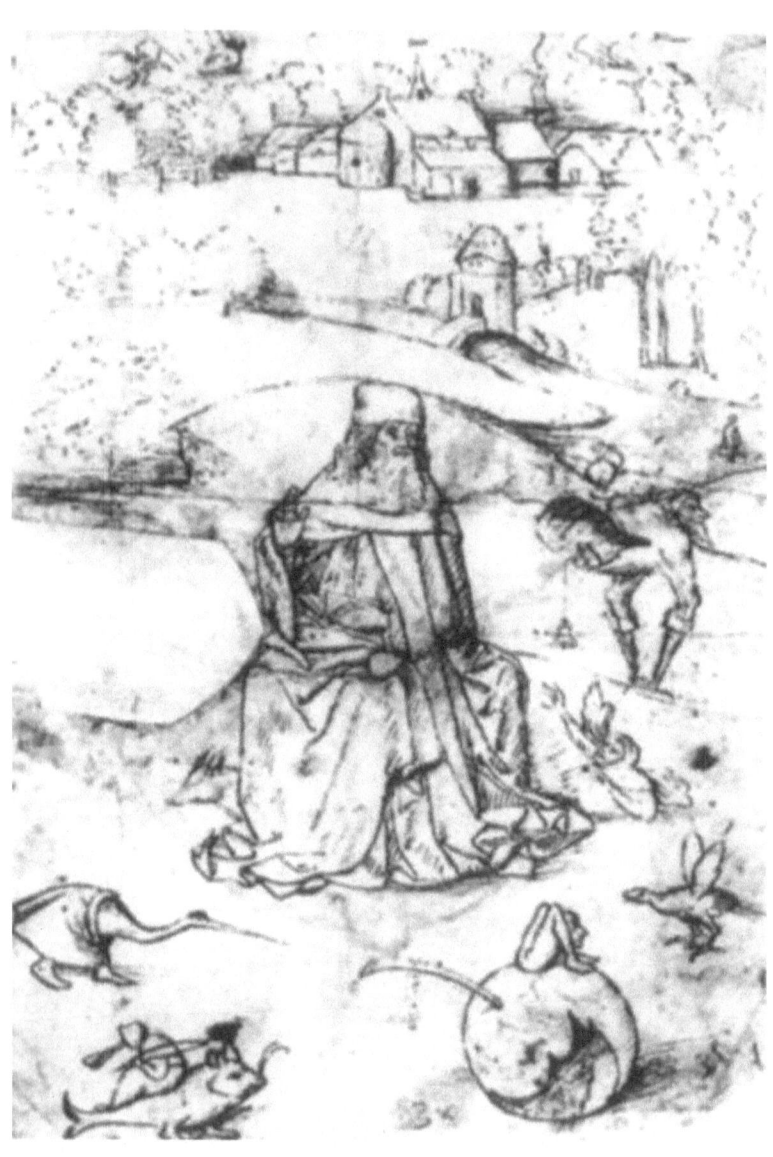

Temptation of St Anthony, Pen and bistre, 257 x 175 mm

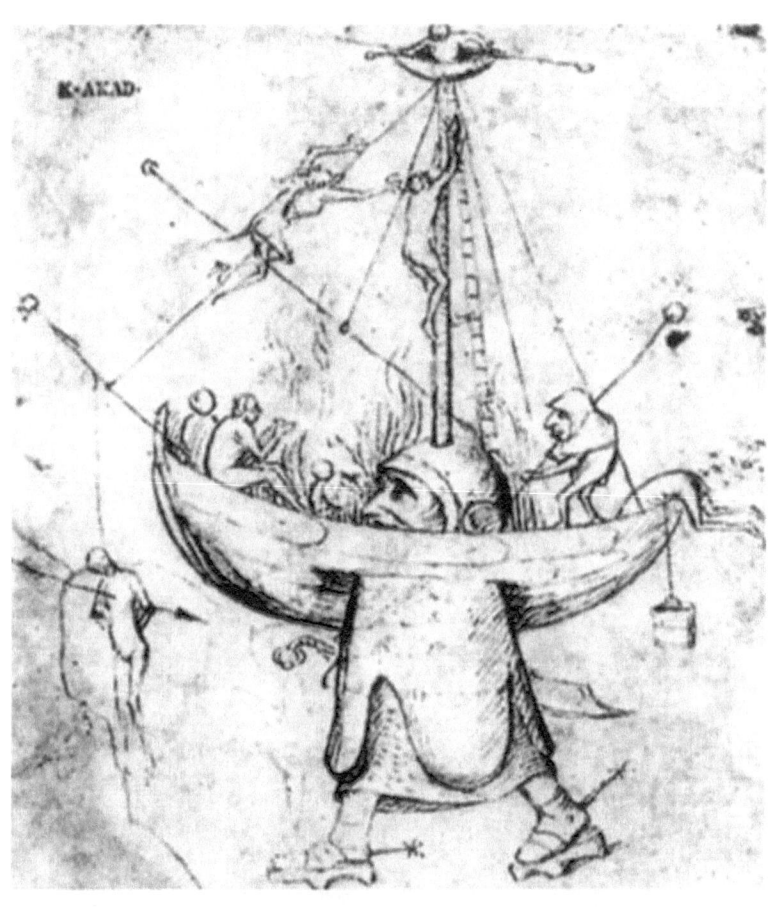

The Ship of Fools in Flames, Pen and bistre, 176 x 153 mm

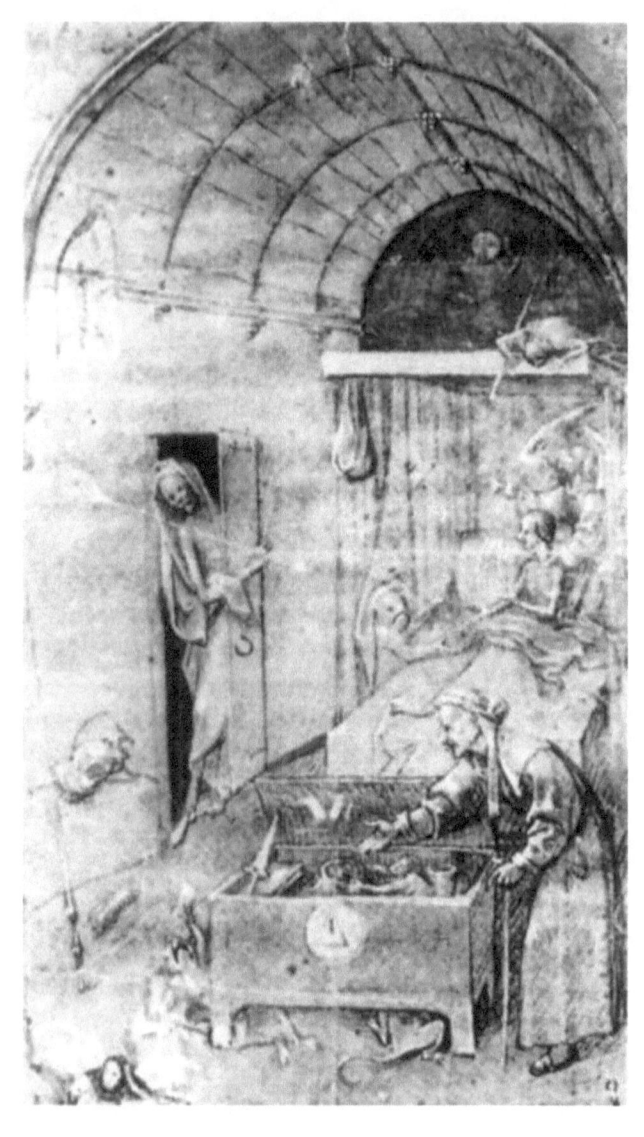

Death and the Miser, Drawing, 256 x 149 mm

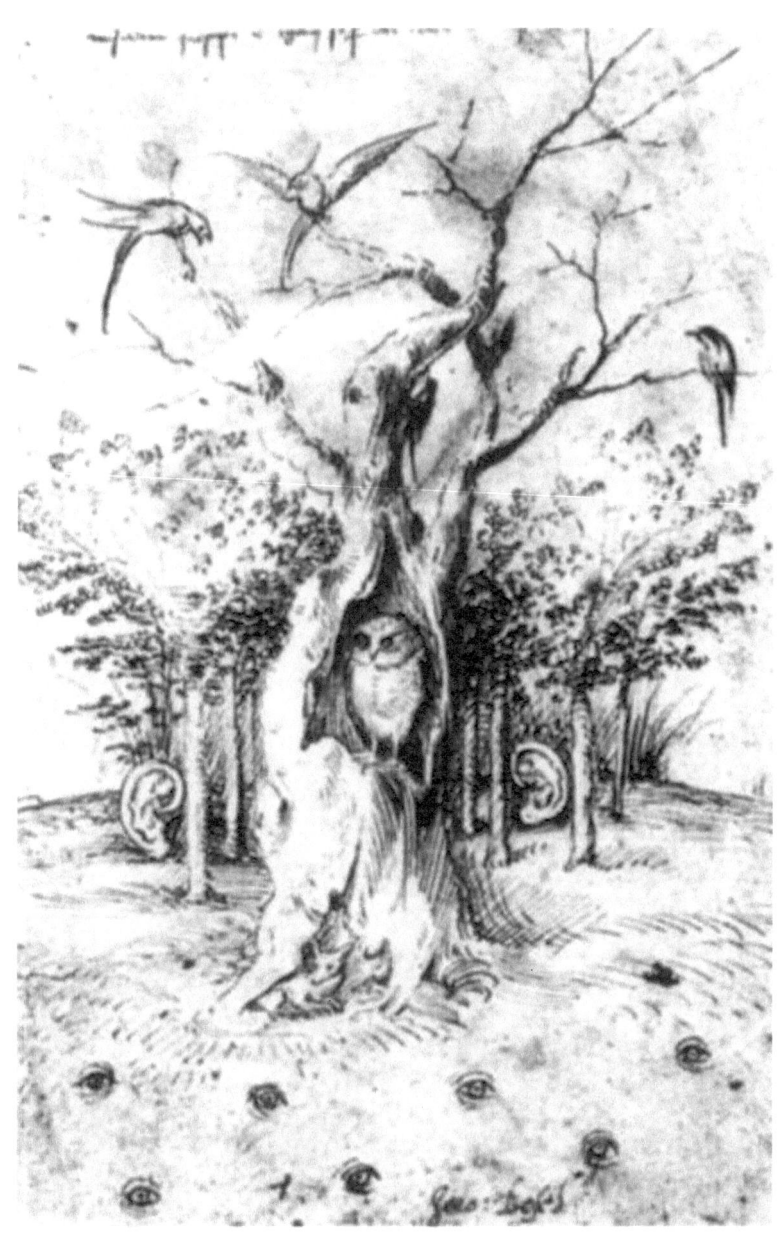

The Hearing Forest and the Seeing Field, Pen and
bistre, 202 x 127 mm

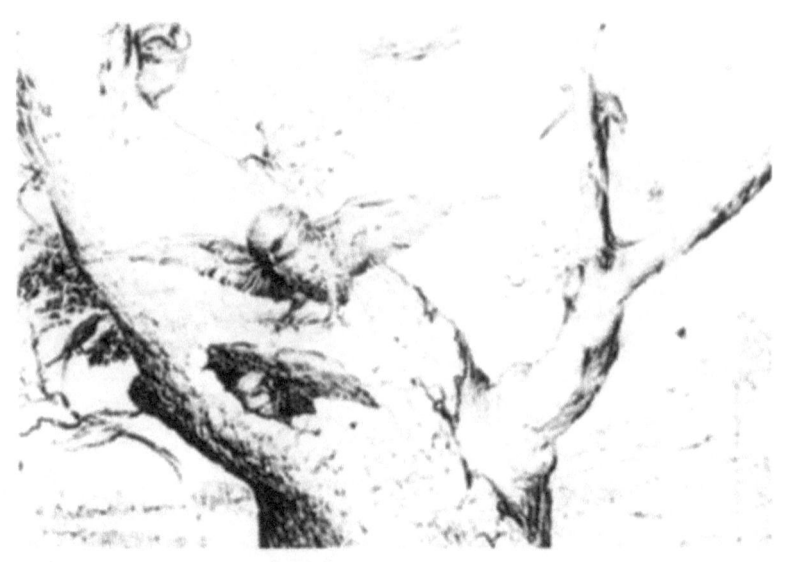

Nest of Owls, Pen and bistre, 140 x 196 mm

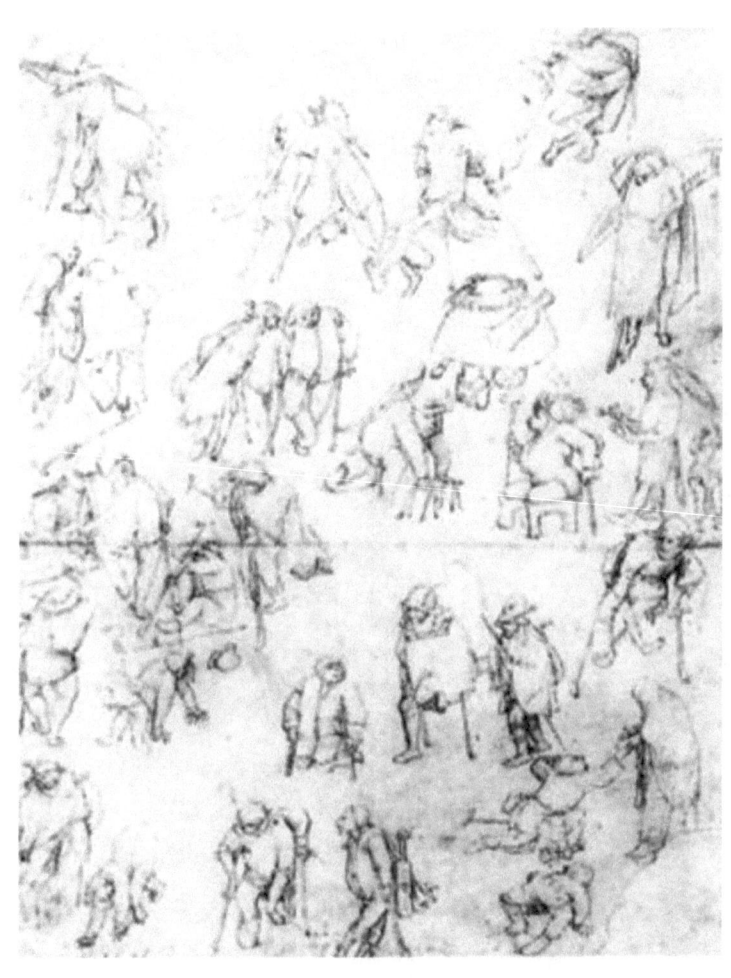

Beggars, Pen and bistre, 285 x 205 mm

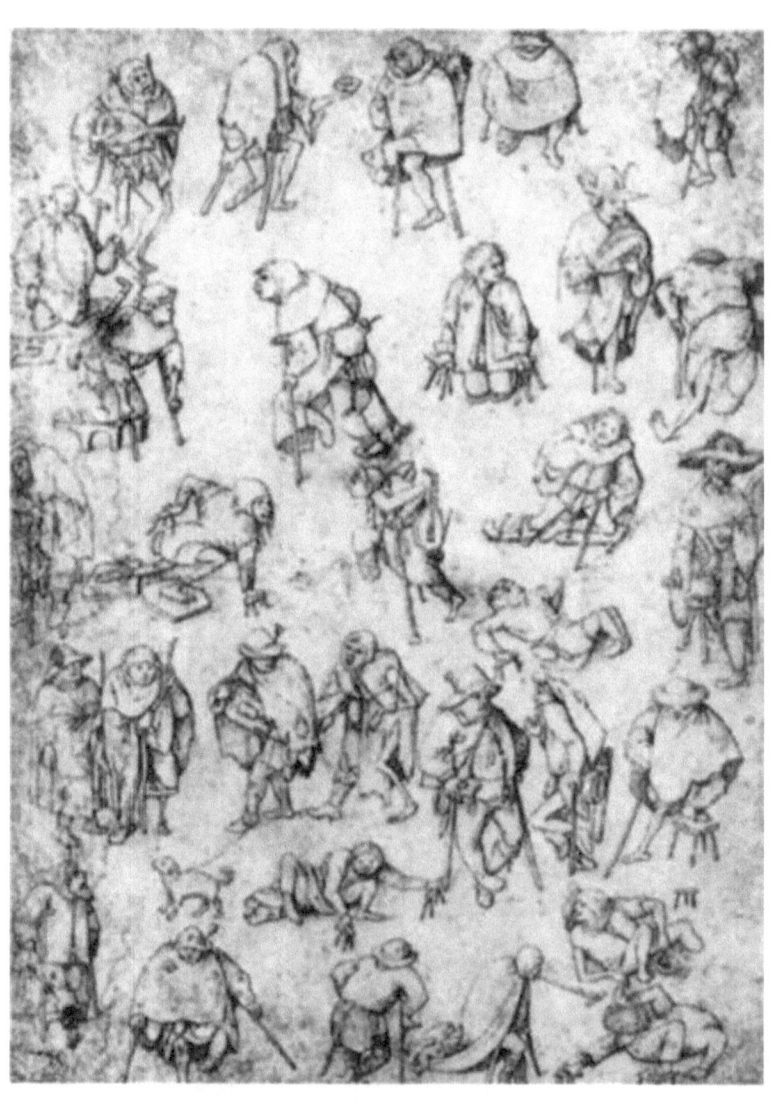

Beggars and Cripples, Pen and bistre, 264 x 198 mm

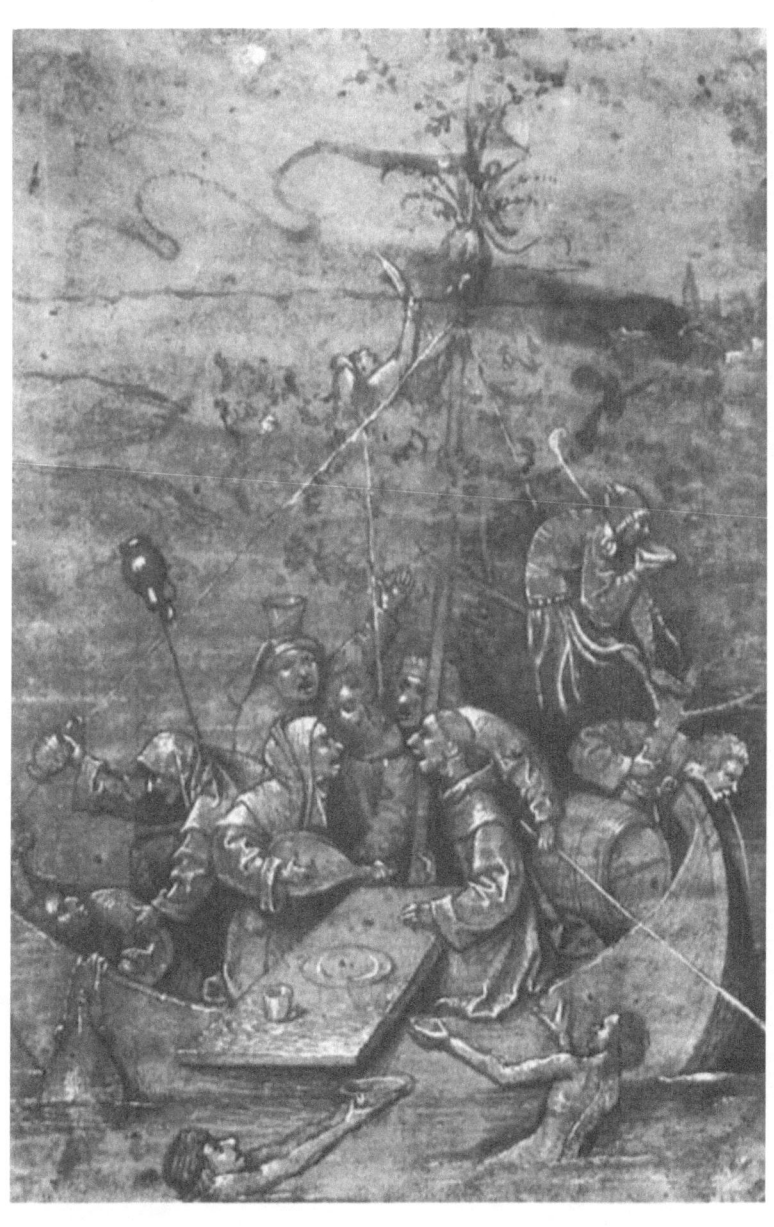

The Ship of Fools (study), Wash on gray paper

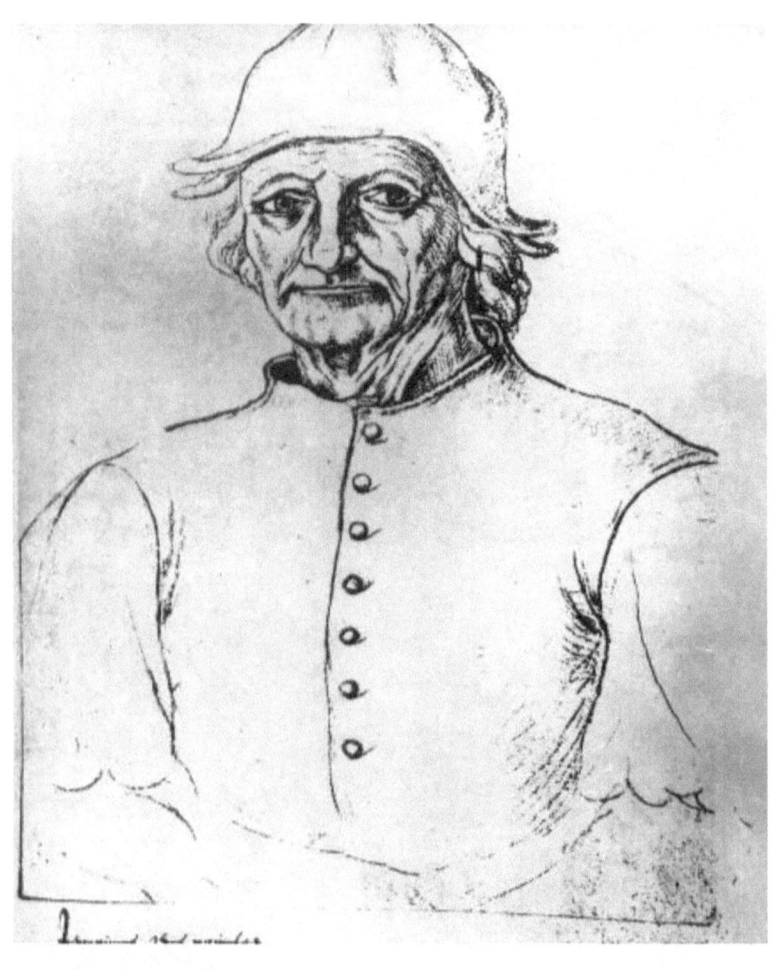

Portrait of Hieronymus Bosch, Pencil and sanguine, 410 x 280 mm

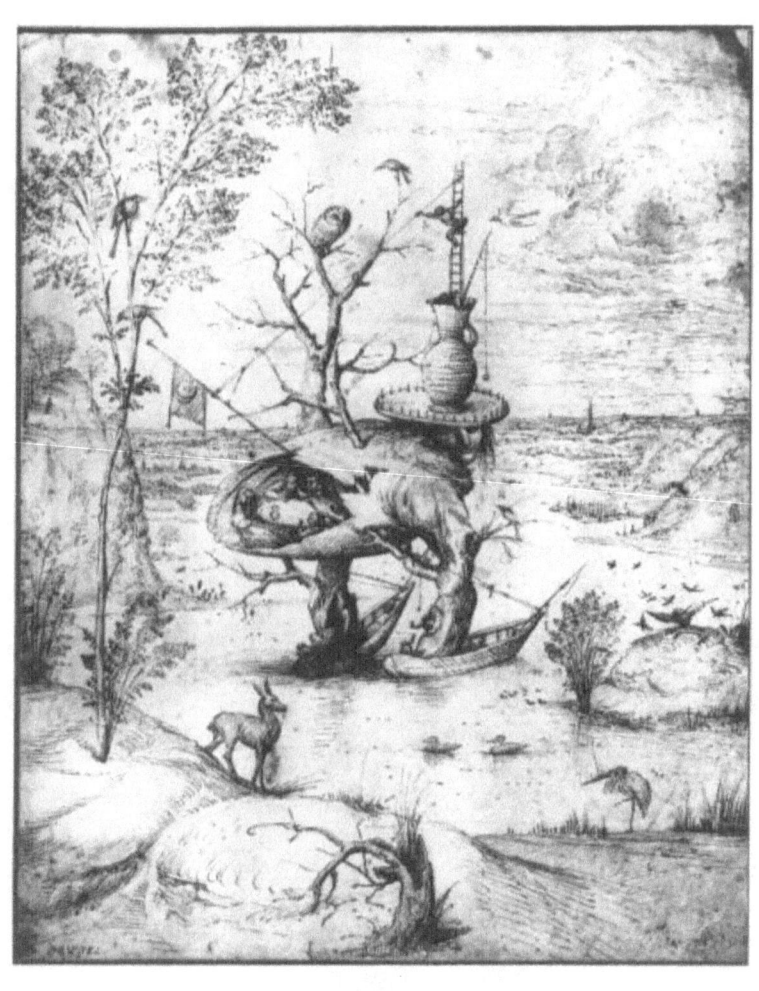

Tree-Man, Pen and bistre, 277 x 211 mm

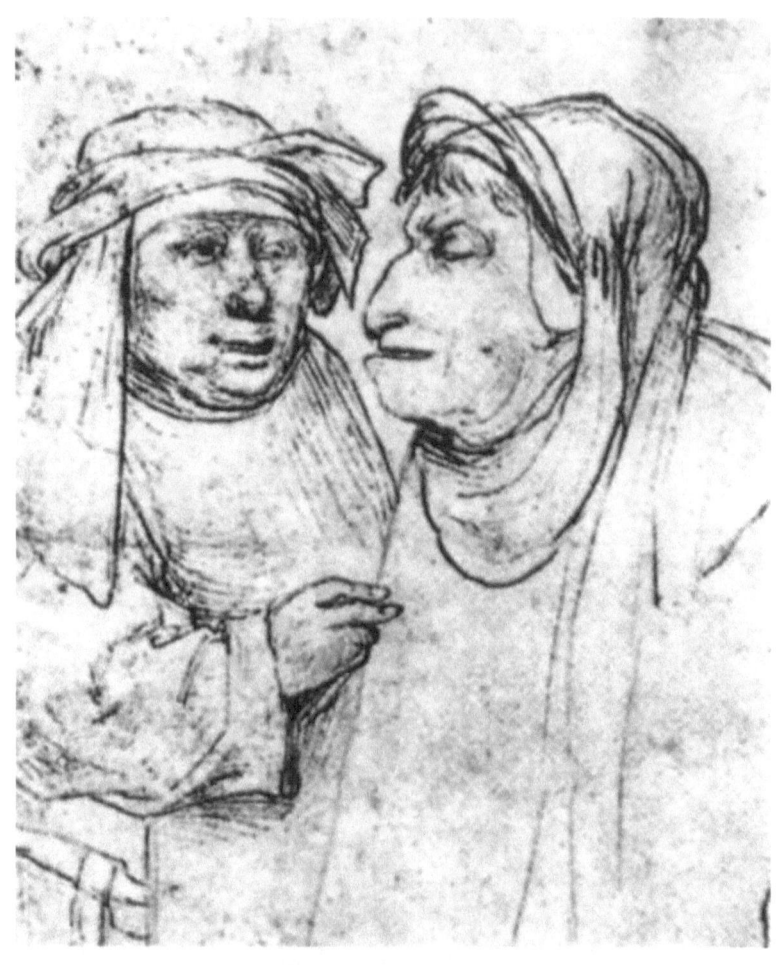

Two Caricatured Heads, Pen and bistre, 133 x 100 mm

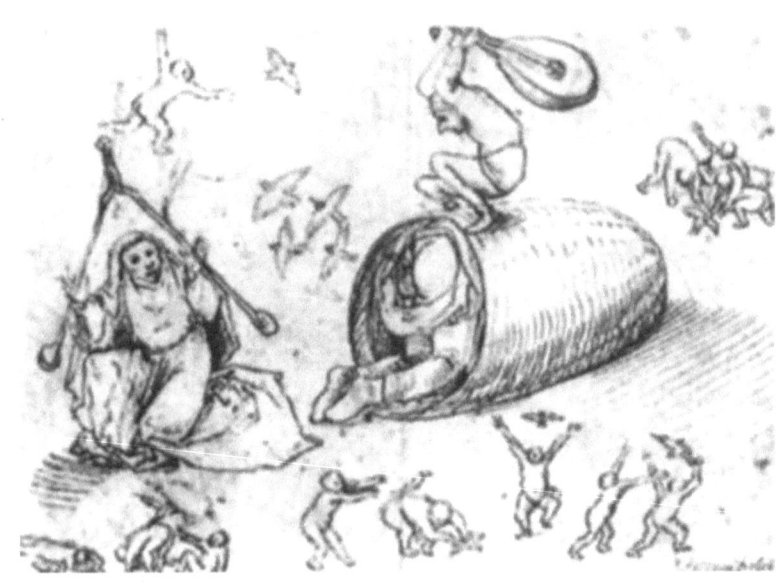

Beehive and Witches, Pen and bistre, 192 x 270 mm

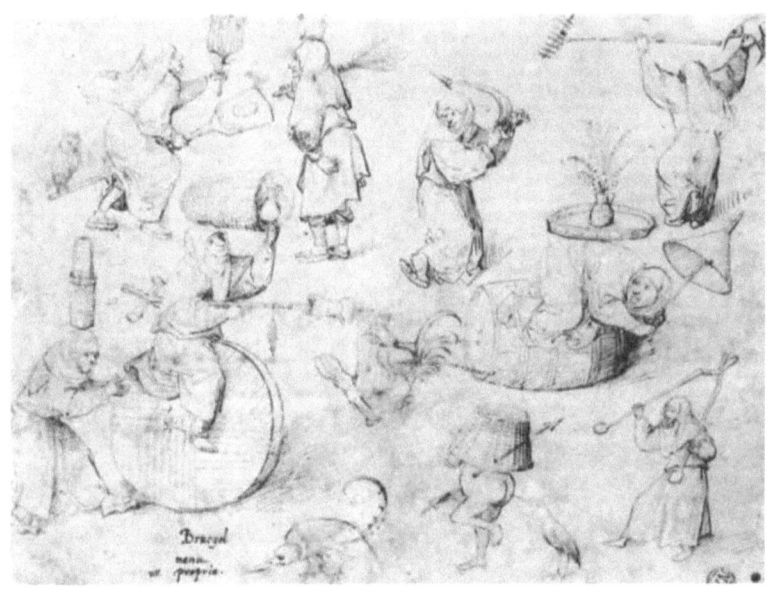

Witches, Pen and bistre, 203 x 264 mm

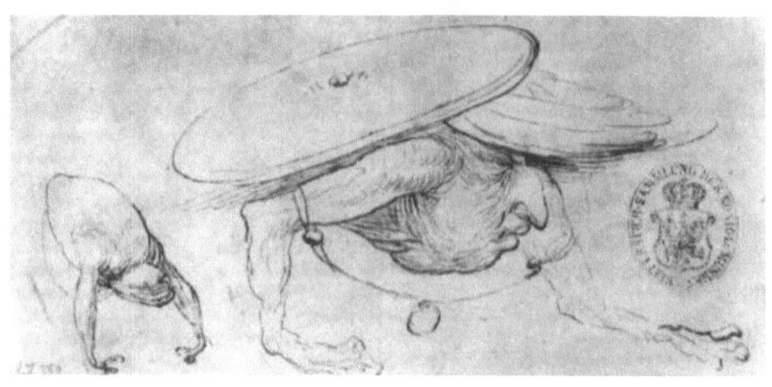

Studies of Monsters, Pen drawing, 86 x 162 mm

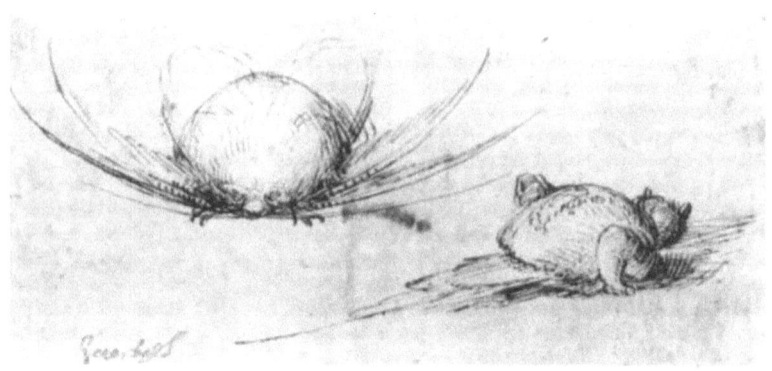

Animal studies, Pen drawing, 86 x 182 mm

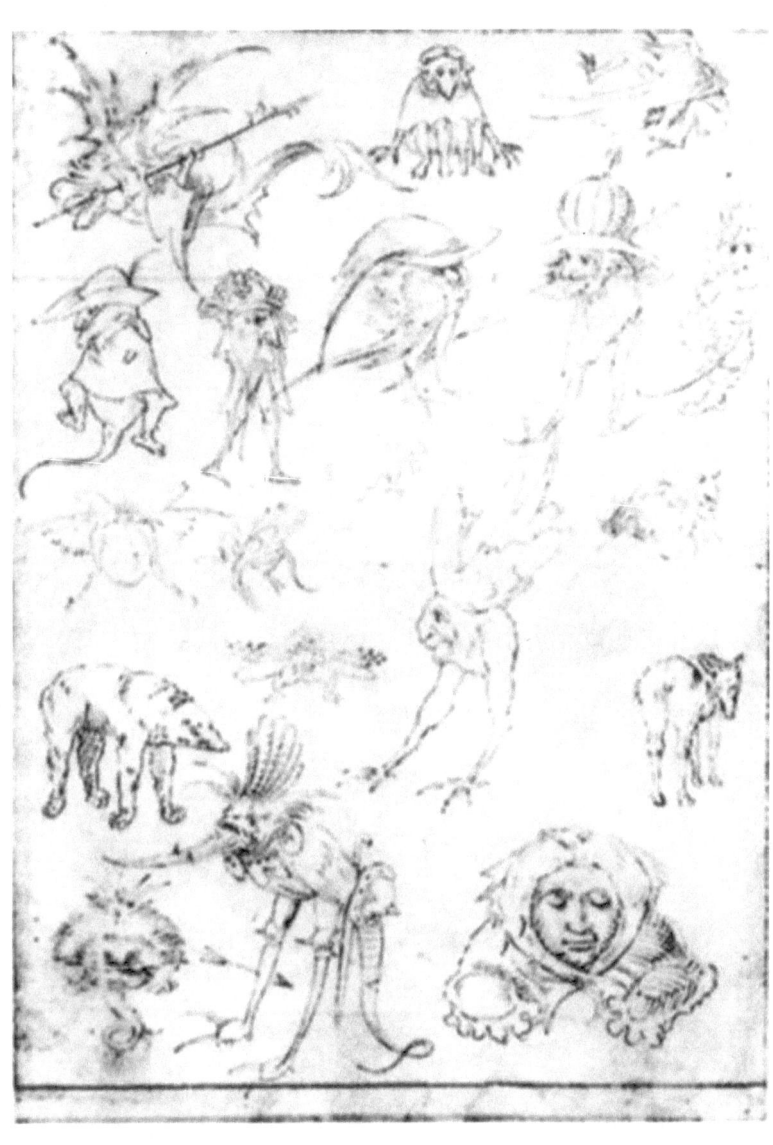

Studies of Monsters, Pen and bistre, 318 x 210 mm

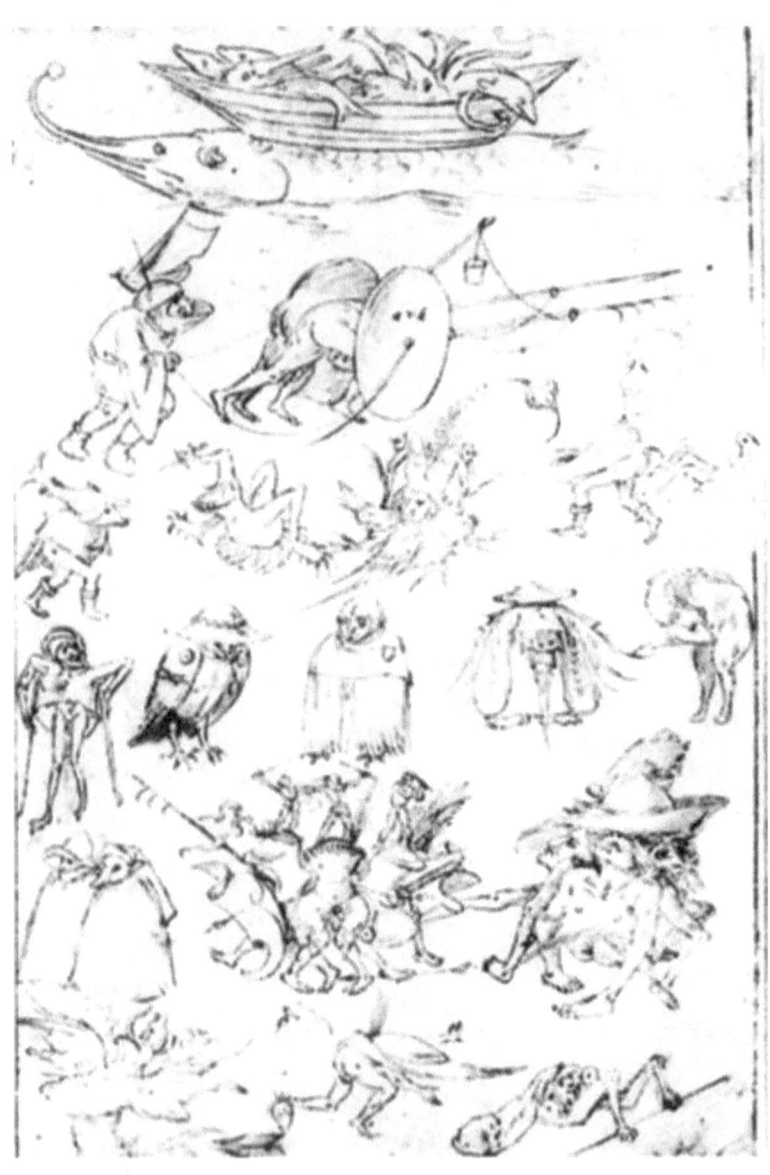

Studies of Monsters, Pen and bistre, 318 x 210 mm

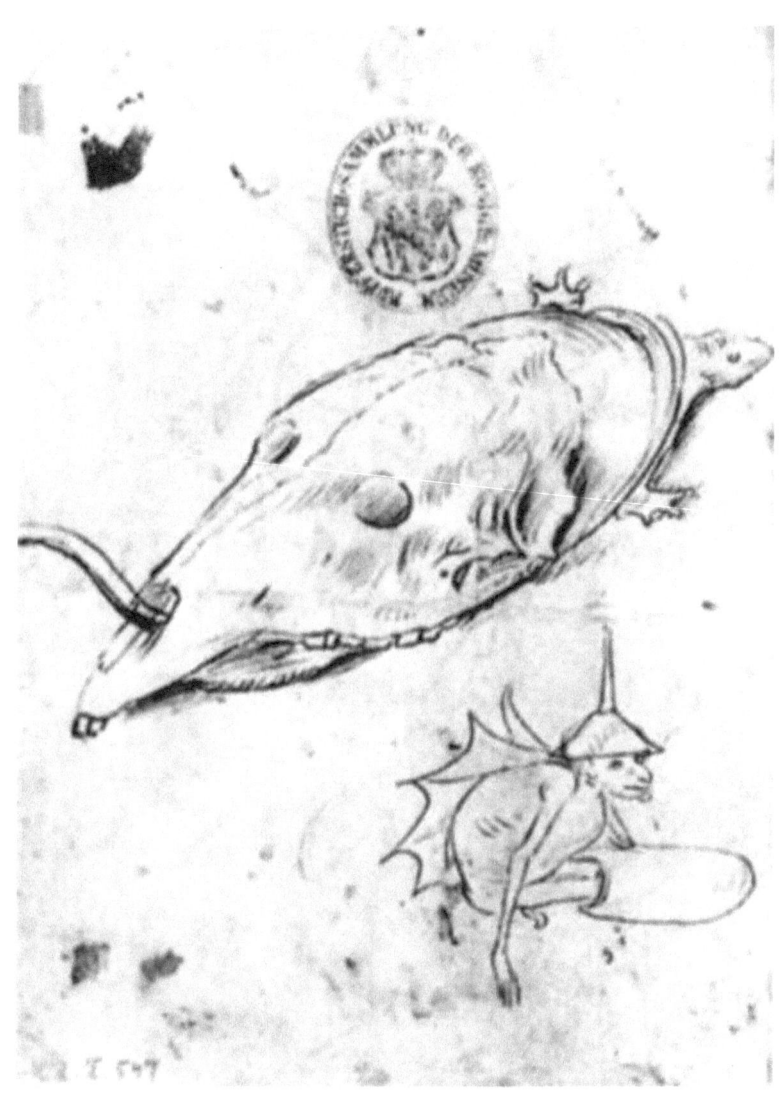

Two Monsters, Pen and bistre, 164 x 116 mm

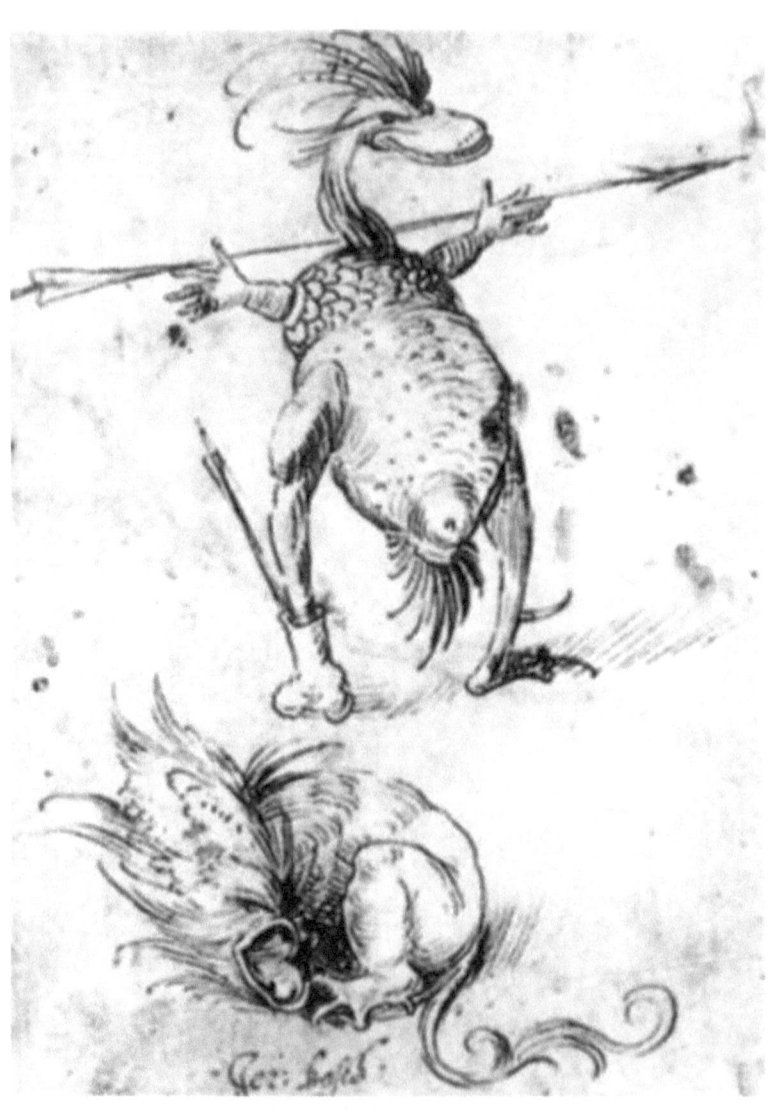

Two Monsters, Pen and bistre, 164 x 116 mm

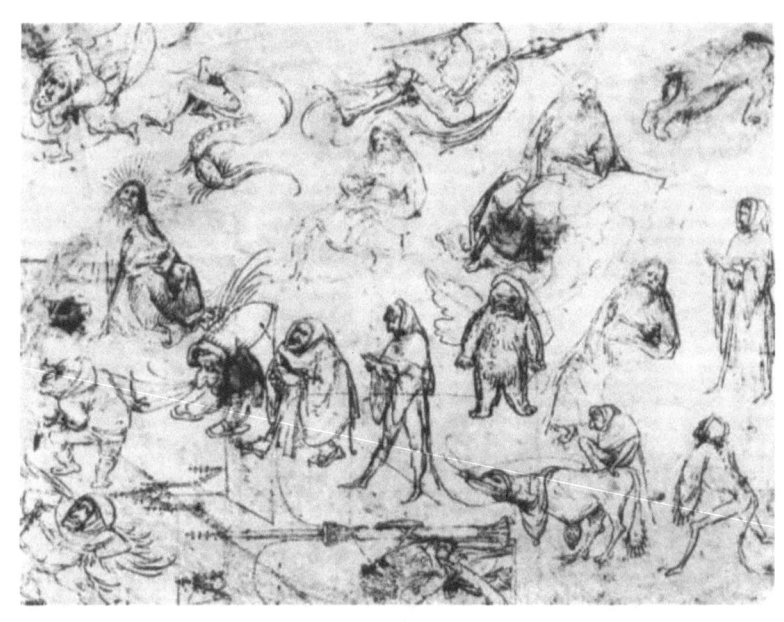

Studies, Pen and bistre, 205 x 263 mm

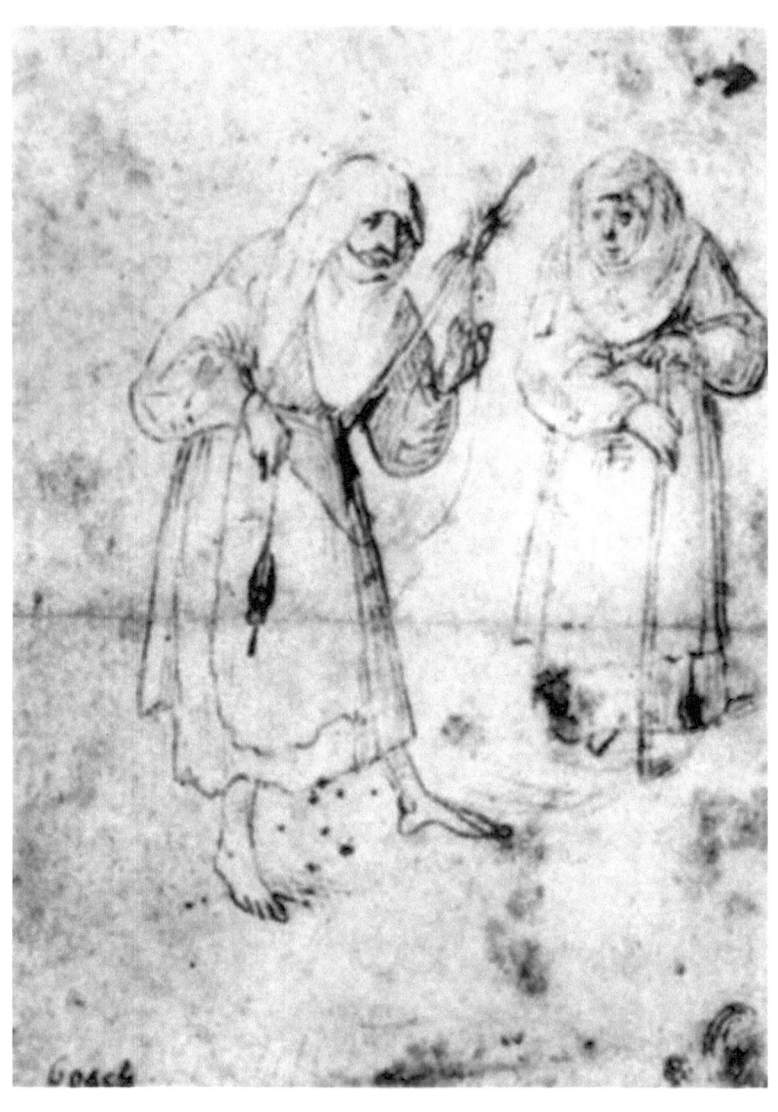

Two Witches, Pen and bistre, 125 x 85 mm

www.ingramcontent.com/pod-product-compliance
Lightning Source LLC
Chambersburg PA
CBHW020909180526
45163CB00007B/2675